be calm.

be calm.

proven techniques to
STOP ANXIETY NOW

JILL P. WEBER, PhD

ALTHEA
PRESS

peace for all

Interior and Cover Designer: Jamison Spittler
Editor: Camille Hayes
Production Editor: Erum Khan
Author photo © Stacy Vaeth Photography

ISBN: Print 978-1-64152-208-3 | eBook 978-1-64152-209-0

R1

Contents

Quick-Start Guide

This book provides a variety of strategies and techniques that have proven effective at reducing anxiety and its most troubling symptoms. Any of the strategies you choose to practice will help your anxiety overall, but I've divided them up here based on which type of symptom they target. This Quick-Start Guide will navigate you straight to the set of strategies that will help you deal with acute symptom flare-ups and anxiety-producing situations.

Section I: Feelings

Turn to the strategies starting on page 20 if you're feeling strong emotional or physical symptoms of anxiety.

- Anger/irritability
- Sadness
- Hopelessness/ despair
- Insomnia
- Mood swings
- Racing heart
- Shortness of breath
- Dizziness
- Stomach upset

Section II: Behavior

Go to page 87 if your anxiety is making you behave in ways that you don't like or that are causing you problems. Section II will be helpful when your anxiety causes you to:

- Avoid activities you used to enjoy
- Avoid certain people
- Frequently cancel plans
- Call in sick to avoid stressful events like presentations
- Feel unable to do routine things like drive or go to the store
- Behave uncharacteristically in anxiety-provoking situations, e.g., you don't approach or talk to your friends when you're at a party

Section III: Thoughts

Starting on page 153, you'll find strategies to help diminish the inaccurate or unhelpful thinking that preoccupies the mind when you're caught up in anxiety. These thought-focused strategies will help if you're experiencing:

- Chronic worry
- Repetitive or racing thoughts
- Catastrophic (worst-case scenario) thinking
- Self-defeating thoughts (e.g., "I suck at this, so I might as well give up.")
- Irrational beliefs (e.g., "If I don't drive back home to check the oven, my house will burn down.")

Welcome

Everyone feels anxious at some point! I have worked with anxious clients for the past 15 years in my practice as a clinical psychologist. Some come to me believing that their anxious feelings can improve. Others enter therapy reluctantly, mostly convinced that nothing will ever reduce their panic symptoms, avoidance behavior, or worried thoughts. People who improve typically have two things in common:

1. A part of them, no matter how small, believes they can get better.

2. They learn, and put to work, effective anxiety-reducing strategies.

Simply opening this book and reading this far shows that some part of you believes your anxious symptoms can get better. And if you're willing to engage with this material and give serious thought to the impact anxiety has on your life, there's a part of you that *wants* to get better. Take heart; you already have all you need to start managing your anxiety symptoms and living a happier, more fulfilling life.

How to Use This Book

Psychology is a young science, and there's still quite a bit we don't know. However, we *do* know how to treat anxiety. Most people who consistently use the psychological tools in this book will find relief. My clients who use these methods tell me that although they are still aware of their worried thoughts, those thoughts no longer have the same power over them. So instead of feeling as if the waves in the ocean are pulling them under and they have to fight for dear life, they realize they can float—even in a stormy sea. They ride out the tempest by using their tools and knowing that the waves will eventually subside and the sea will be calm again.

The strategies in this book are simple to implement. They are all evidence based, meaning research has proven their effectiveness. They come from cognitive behavioral therapy (CBT), acceptance and commitment therapy (ACT, pronounced like the word *act*), and mindfulness practices.

It's not necessary to go through the book from start to finish in order to improve. You likely have not experienced the whole range of possible anxiety symptoms described here, so you may choose to skip some sections, depending on what you're experiencing. Although this is not a workbook, it is full of practical strategies and instructions for how to implement them. In each of the nine main chapters you'll see sections titled "Go Deeper," which are suggestions on how to take the strategies to the next level. (You'll need a notebook or journal for these.) The "Go Deeper" strategies are optional, but they are a great way to maximize your results.

Getting Started

Keep a notebook or journal handy so you can jot down your thoughts about the strategies as you try them out. Your notes will help you reflect on what you're learning and how your new skills can help you better cope with anxiety. The more you practice and write about the strategies, the faster they'll become automatic responses to your anxiety triggers.

Once you have your notebook and are ready to start, take a moment to think about your schedule. Consider how/when you want to work on this material and when you can best fit it into your general routine. To really get up to speed with your new skills, daily practice is the way to go—even if you can set aside only a few minutes. The point is, give some thought to how you're going to integrate this book into your routine.

If you're in the middle of an acute symptom flare-up, I encourage you to go directly to the relevant section. So, for example, if you're consumed by worried or intrusive thinking, start with section III, "Thoughts" (page 146). If your anxiety is causing you to avoid important events or people, you may want to start with section II, "Behavior" (page 78). If you're struggling with your feelings or physical health, start with section I (page 12).

To reach longer-term goals of sustained peace of mind and inner calm, consider breaking the material down into small, doable steps so you eventually work through the entire book, at the pace that suits your life.

CHAPTER ONE

Is Anxiety Running Your Life?

Why We Struggle with Anxiety

A snake on a hiking trail, or a gun in your face, or any direct threat to your well-being will trigger your fight-or-flight response. When this happens, the sympathetic nervous system releases a cascade of hormones, in particular adrenaline and epinephrine. These stress hormones very rapidly cause a series of changes in your body, including increased blood pressure and heart rate, slowed digestion, tunnel vision, shaking, and increased muscle tension. All this prepares you for a full-throttle physical response to the danger. These changes come together in an instant, to create a singular focus on *survival*.

When anxiety is appropriate—as in the case of the snake or the gun—this physiological response is normal, because it prepares us to respond to the potential threat.

Even when the perceived danger *isn't* life-threatening, anxiety can still be helpful. For example, a student might need to achieve a certain score on a test in order to be accepted to medical school. His anxiety motivates him to study, take a test prep course, and spend considerable time on practice exams. The fear of failure can energize and focus him for the hard work ahead. Or a person driving on a busy highway suddenly experiences increased heart rate and blood flow when she sees someone screech to a halt in the lane next to her. The immediate increase in heart rate prepares her for action, so she can steer toward safety if she needs to. These kinds of anxiety responses may not be saving our lives, but they are adaptive and keep things running smoothly.

Anxiety becomes a problem when a person's fight-or-flight response is triggered by cues that are not threatening at all—either physically or otherwise. For instance, the person who obsessively worries about their health even though tests have ruled out a medical condition. This person is unable to be present with the people around them because they're constantly preoccupied by what might or might not be going on medically. Or take the person who fears using public bathrooms and eventually avoids all business travel in order to not have to confront this fear. If travel is necessary for work, this person's career will be limited or ended by what is, at its core, an irrational fear.

Anxiety isn't just a problem of overreacting to things happening around us; our anxiety response can be triggered by things that exist only in our minds. This happens when we worry about and anticipate what-ifs and worst-case scenarios, which may never come to be. Consider the person who feels insecure and frets relentlessly about the possibility of doing something wrong socially and being embarrassed. Eventually their social world becomes smaller and smaller. They may no longer go to social events and may even stop opening up to people they've known for a long time.

If you're holding this book, you likely struggle with anxiety in some way. But you may still have questions about whether or not anxiety is a problem for you, or about how serious a problem it is. There are some general ways to assess if you're dealing with problematic anxiety, or just the normal fears that arise in life from time to time.

Anxiety is *adaptive* when it comes in response to an in-the-moment fear of risk in your immediate environment. Anxiety is *maladaptive* when it becomes a chronic state of tension, worry, and/or avoidance behavior, all of which negatively impacts your life and functioning.

The table on the next page describes the differences between normal fear and problematic anxiety.

FEAR	ANXIETY
Fear is present-focused and generally rational in that it's responding to a threatening situation or event.	Anxiety is future-focused and can easily become irrational because it is untethered from real events. Your imagination continually calls up what-if scenarios.
You're in the here and now. There is a fire in the house, and you're figuring out how to put it out. Once the fire is out, your fear subsides.	You feel worry and discomfort even though you are not in immediate danger. No clear threat is present and there is no clear way to solve the concern.
Fear comes from real threats in the outside world, e.g., job loss; medical diagnosis; illness of a loved one; threat of being physically harmed; wanting to do well on a specific task, such as a speech or an exam; wanting to make a good impression on new acquaintances.	For the most part, anxiety isn't created by the outside world; it's created by your mind. You worry about possibilities that may or may not happen, such as: "What if they don't like me?" "What if the plane crashes?" "What if I can't leave the movie theater?" "What if they hate me?" "What if I have a panic attack?" "What if I make a fool of myself?"

What We Can Do About It

The Anxiety and Depression Association of America estimates that 40 million people suffer from anxiety disorders, which are the most common issues that bring people to therapy. Thanks to decades of research, we know a good deal about how to treat them. In fact, anxiety symptoms of all kinds are very responsive to treatment, offering anxiety sufferers long-term relief. This book gives you access to some of the same tools I use in my practice to help people struggling with all types of anxiety symptoms.

The techniques in this book are taken mainly from three scientifically tested and proven-effective interventions. As a clinician and also as someone who struggles with anxiety, I have personally found relief using these specific approaches, and so have my clients. I believe you will, too.

What research and experience have shown me is that a combined approach of examining your thoughts, accepting (not necessarily liking!) anxiety as a part of your life, and learning to be more present in the here and now are the essential keys to reducing anxiety and living a more peaceful life.

Having anxious thoughts becomes a self-perpetuating cycle that creates more anxiety. We'll use cognitive behavioral therapy to examine and change your thoughts. Strategies from acceptance and commitment therapy will help you behave in a manner, and ultimately live a life, that matches your core values and desires, regardless of your mood or anxious symptoms.

As you grow to accept that we all suffer sometimes, you'll find there's more room for you to separate from your battle with anxiety. Through practicing the mindfulness strategies throughout each chapter, you'll be more easily able to bring your thoughts back to the here and now. As you learn ways to observe and distance yourself, even if only slightly, from your anxious experiences, you will be less overwhelmed and more able to experience joy and pleasure in your life now.

Habits and Neuroplasticity

Struggling with anxiety can be so demoralizing that we give up. Similar to traits like height or eye color, people who struggle with anxiety can start to believe that they were born anxious and there's nothing they can do about it. However, the reality is that changes in our environment, along with learning new skills, have a significant impact on anxiety and can lessen anxious symptoms over time.

Neuroscience shows that neuronal growth and structural changes in the brain occur as the result of new experiences, and also as the result of how you think and behave. A real-life example of this would be if you decided you wanted to change your habit of snacking right before bed. Perhaps you've eaten chips or crackers before bed for years, and you decide to substitute sliced vegetables. The plan is solid and you're ready to go. However, you're unlikely to be successful in changing this habit if you substitute your chips for veggies only once a week or every couple of weeks. On the other hand, if you consistently eat sliced veggies every night of the week, or even just most nights of the week, your brain will adjust and the new habit will take hold.

When you repeat a new behavior enough (which continually fires the same neuronal pathway), the new experience becomes a part of your brain's system on a chemical level. This phenomenon is called neuronal plasticity, or sometimes brain plasticity.

Tap Your Growth Potential

People just like you, with similar symptoms and levels of anxiety, have triumphed over anxiety largely because they believed they could. Recognize if you send yourself self-defeating messages, such as telling yourself no amount of work will lessen your symptoms. Just having these thoughts can hinder your progress.

Take this assessment to see how much you believe in your ability to grow and have the internal peace you deserve and desire. If you answer yes often, let's plan to cultivate your capacity to believe that freedom from anxiety is possible.

1. When I'm told some way of thinking or behaving will help my anxiety, I zone out, think nothing can help, or that this person doesn't get it.

2. If I have to work hard at something, I feel like something is wrong with me.

3. I want to stay just as I am, but I am unhappy where I am.

4. I don't believe the anxious aspects of my personality that bother me are changeable through learning and new experience.

5. Most of what I do is to survive and get through the day and less about what I want.

6. I'd rather stay stuck in anxiety than learn new ways of coping.

As you work your way through the strategies in this book you will likely start to believe in your ability to grow. Revisit this assessment from time to time to see the progress you're making in believing in yourself. In time, you will look back and feel both surprised and proud of your growth.

WRAP-UP

- Anxiety is a normal bodily response to threat.

- Feeling fearful about something in your immediate environment is adaptive.

- Imagining what-if situations that may or may not come to pass is maladaptive.

- Anxiety responds to treatment; you can and will get better.

- The brain is able to grow and change structurally as the result of new experiences over time.

- Believing that reducing anxiety is in your control and hard work will pay off makes all the difference. You can do this!

feelings

Imagine a triangle with "Feelings" in one corner, "Behavior" in another, and "Thoughts" in the third. These represent the three main paths to change, which lead to relief from a wide range of anxiety symptoms. This book is divided into these three main sections, too.

A change in one corner of the triangle will affect the other two. If you change your emotions—like learning strategies to calm your fear and anxiety in social situations—then you will likely change your thoughts ("When I calm my anxiety, I can contribute to the conversation and people will like me") and your behavior (you stop avoiding social activities). Simply put, if you're trying to effect change, you can start with any corner of the triangle.

In this first section, we will look at your anxious feelings, both emotional (sadness, anger, mood swings, helplessness) and physical (shortness of breath, heart palpitations, insomnia). You'll learn better ways of dealing with your feelings and how to overcome avoiding or

```
                    THOUGHTS



        FEELINGS    ←——————→    BEHAVIORS
```

pushing your emotions away. We will also see how the
stress of anxiety can lead to unpleasant physical side
effects, such as digestion problems, racing heart, and
chronic headaches. Together we will uncover what lurks
underneath your anxiety, which may be the most important factor when life is disrupted by anxiety.

CHAPTER TWO

Your Emotions

Are You Suppressing Your Emotions?

A few years back I took a genetic test to determine if I was at heightened risk for developing certain cancers. I did this at the urging of my doctor, who rightfully promoted prevention over treatment. This thinking made sound sense to me, and given that I don't have a family history of cancer, I believed I would get the reassurance of longevity. I was shocked when I was told I had an 80 percent lifetime risk of developing breast cancer. (The average risk is 12 percent.) I distinctly remember thinking, "This can't be happening; there must be a mistake in the test." The information was too overwhelming for me to process emotionally so I pushed it away.

As a result, I became obsessively focused on negative thoughts about other aspects of my life. I was unable to sleep most nights, overwhelmed by worries and what-ifs. What I wasn't doing was acknowledging my profound sadness and grief. Once I started to get in touch with the vulnerability I felt, the anxiety became easier to manage.

The more we avoid or push away our emotions, the more anxious we become. This self-defeating process is a learned habit that actually worsens anxiety over time, in part because it reinforces anxious thoughts and anxiety-driven behavior. This happens because to keep the unwanted emotion at bay, we have to continually work at avoidance. Over time, keeping up this avoidance becomes something else we're anxious about. When we, despite our best efforts, drop our guard even for a moment, the pushed-away emotions come flooding in and we again anxiously push them away. On this merry-go-round the original negative emotion goes unaddressed and we remain ill at ease and hypervigilant.

How Do You Feel Right Now?

As you learn to better identify your feelings you will gain greater emotional control. This means you will be less prone to intense emotional reactions, such as panic attacks, emotional meltdowns, blowups, crying spells, and worried thinking. Plus, knowing what you're feeling means you can address the real issue and feel better. When you're upset or aware you're experiencing anxiety, use the following chart to help you label the deeper feeling(s) that may be underneath your anxiety.

EMOTIONS	PHYSICAL/ BODILY SENSATIONS	LABELS TO DESCRIBE YOUR EXPERIENCE
LOVE	Calm body, relaxed muscles, sense of peace and well-being	Sense of comfort, safety, comfort with another, passion, sexual longing
PLEASURE	Feel-good hormones released, increased energy, lack of physical pain, excited body	Delight, joy, vivaciousness, contentment, mastery, feeling lost in the moment, not thinking about the future or the past
ANGER	Tense body, clenched jaw, tightened muscles, increased body temperature, feeling of pressure behind the eyes	Feeling unfairly treated or disrespected by others or the world as a whole, outrage, rage, feeling the self is not valued
SADNESS	Desire to remain still, feeling of lethargy and lack of energy, difficulty getting your body to move	Loss, grief, hopelessness, rejection, feeling defeated or unwanted, feeling bad about the self
ANXIETY	Stress hormones released in the brain, muscle tension, restlessness, increased heartbeat, sweating, shortness of breath, stomachache	Being worried or fearful, feeling threatened by something in the environment or within a relationship (fear of losing a relationship), being in high-alert/vigilant/survival mode
GUILT	Stomachache, aching muscles, feeling that you can't be physically at ease	Feeling like a "bad" person, feeling destructive, feeling you should be punished
SHAME	Burning sensation on face, cheeks flushing, stomach sinking	Embarrassment, humiliation, exposure as a fraud, fearing a flaw will be revealed to another or the public

ACTION URGES	EVOLUTIONARY SIGNIFICANCE
Desire to be with the person, to bond with the other, to make sure the other is okay	Love bonds couples, children, families, and tribes. It is the glue that connects people.
Urge to smile, laugh, talk more with others, and reveal more about yourself	Pleasure is a tonic for negative emotions and motivates us to do certain things in order to experience more pleasure.
Urge to be aggressive or harm another, urge to yell or throw something	Anger cues the body to self-protect through physical force, self-assertion, or boundary setting.
Urge to cry or sit still in one place, lack of motivation, urge to dwell on what you did to cause the loss	Sadness is protective in that it allows the self to mark time while grief and problem-solving can take place.
Urge to be vigilant, replay events in one's mind, predict future events, desire to control the threat, flee, or be busy	Anxiety triggers adrenaline, which puts the body into high alert, primed for action and protection.
Urge to make amends, to be a "better" person, to berate oneself	Guilt keeps people in line with societal laws and norms designed for protecting people.
Urge to flee the situation, to become invisible and hide oneself	Shame signifies social status in a group and keeps people in accordance with group expectations.

STRATEGY: EXPRESSING YOURSELF

When you're feeling strong emotions, finding a way to express those feelings can go a long way toward helping you move through them. There are countless benefits in talking about our feelings with another person. For example, I see it over and over again in my practice that a person comes into a therapy session feeling upset or anxious. They allow themselves to talk about their feelings for 50 minutes, and they leave feeling significantly better. Many often say, "That's too easy. How can merely talking make such a difference?" The answer is that the act of talking, labeling, and expressing moves emotional information from your emotional brain to your frontal lobe, which helps you better understand yourself and feel more in control of your emotions, which makes you feel better.

Choose a person with whom you can discuss your feelings. Try to look the person in the eyes while expressing yourself, because maintaining eye contact with a supportive connection will further soothe your nervous system.

Emotional relief can come by talking with others with whom you have very little intimacy or contact, such as a therapist or support group. Even talking online with someone you don't know that well may help you feel more accepted and less anxious.

Go Deeper

Express Yourself

As you explore the feelings table and begin talking about your feelings, write down in your notebook the emotions that seem to come up for you the most. Record one or two of these primary emotions. This isn't a writing test so don't worry about your writing style, spelling, or punctuation. Simply ask yourself the following questions:

- How old were you when you first remember feeling this emotion?

- What was the situation? Was that situation at all similar to what you're going through now?

- Did you express what you were feeling to anyone?

- Did anyone comfort you or help you make sense of your feelings?

See if in your writing you can comfort yourself now through self-compassion and self-acceptance. Tell yourself, "It's okay to feel this (your specific emotion)." See if you can let yourself believe that part of the problem is never having allowed yourself to reflect on and accept your deeper emotional experiences.

What's Underneath Anxiety?

When we don't express negative experiences, they become internalized—we try to problem solve the upset in an internal vacuum, which results in overthinking and a sense that we can't turn our mind off. Without a release valve, all those negative, doomsday thoughts just keep bouncing around inside our heads.

Take the example of Zander, a typical patient in my psychotherapy practice, who is grief struck by the death of a loved one. Instead of expressing his feelings and allowing himself to be openly sad, he suppresses his pain. Seemingly out of nowhere Zander finds himself obsessing about the details of the loved one's medical expenses, funeral, and the what-ifs now that the loved one is deceased. Over time, his world becomes smaller and smaller. He is afraid to go out and spends most of his time at home ruminating (working through negative events by mentally replaying them again and again).

Another example is Valentina, who after her divorce, blocks the normal feelings of anger, loss, and sadness and instead becomes obsessively focused on her weight. She replays in her mind what she did or didn't eat that day, plans her next meal, imagines herself larger or smaller. In this way she occupies her mind to avoid confronting the hurt and upset of the divorce. The avoidance only increases the loss she has not fully experienced emotionally, and so she clings more tightly to her unhealthy eating patterns.

If you're a chronically anxious person, you're likely in a habit of suppressing your negative emotions. You may be aware of your anxiety but unwilling to explore what might be under, or driving, the anxiety. As uncomfortable as the anxiety feels, it can still feel easier than managing more threatening emotions, such as anger or sadness or shame or guilt. Let's take a look at how to start doing just that.

STRATEGY: EXPLORING ANGER

If you struggle with anxiety, the moment you feel an ember of anger brewing, you likely blink it away. Anger is adaptive, evolution's way of motivating us to protect ourselves through boundary setting and self-assertion.

1. Build awareness of anger. Notice when your body gets tight, your jaw tenses, or your heart rate increases. Instead of going to your automatic anxious-spiral default, ask yourself, "What feeling might I be resisting right now?" and "What might I be missing?" and "Is anger present?"

2. For 10 minutes, without taking any action, without distracting yourself with your worries, and without self-criticism, tolerate your anger being present.

3. Breathe in and out, simply letting yourself be aware of the anger.

NOTE: *Becoming aware of anger doesn't mean you need to react to it. One client I worked with recognized that when she was starting to become angry her jaw clenched up. Recognizing this anger signal helped her know when she was angry long before it became intense enough to be self-defeating.*

STRATEGY: EXPLORING SADNESS

Many of us will go lots of other places first, even to rage, rather than willingly feel the vulnerability of sadness. This short meditation is a safe way to feel an uncomfortable emotion, by inviting it in rather than feeling overwhelmed by it. By meeting sadness on your terms, you'll have the advantage, and you'll start to learn that you can actually tolerate feeling sad and that it isn't such a threat to you after all.

1. Sit comfortably or lie down on your back. Close your eyes. Allow the tension in your body to release as you breathe in and out.

2. Invite sadness into your conscious awareness; remember moments when you felt sadness.

Consider when sadness was present but was overlooked and unattended to. Review your relationships, experiences, achievements, and various circumstances through the lens of sadness.

3. Now be a gentle, curious observer. Where is the sadness located in your body? Do you feel tenderness in your stomach, behind your eyes, a feeling of fragility or vulnerability? Maybe you can observe an urge to cry or to retreat. Perhaps your heart feels tense or heavy.

4. Recognize when a voice in your head pulls you away. Gently direct your attention back to your sad feelings.

5. Your suffering only wants to know that you see it and that you no longer have to hide and suppress it. Repeat internally, "I see you, sadness. I feel you. I am side by side with you."

6. Feel the sadness as you breathe in. Release the sadness as you breathe out. Notice the feeling as it comes in and how observing it allows it to become less intense.

How Do You Feel About Your Feelings?

We minimize our very real and normal emotions by telling ourselves, "It's bad that I feel this way," or "My negative emotions mean I'm weak," or "What's wrong with me that I feel this way?" or "I'm such a loser because I'm always upset," or "No one will ever love me because my emotions are out of control." When we negatively judge our emotions, we experience double the emotional pain. On top of the original hurt or upset, we feel worthless for having the feeling in the first place.

Telling yourself you're a weak loser for a feeling you can't help but experience is a particularly harsh torment. Take, for example, Tanisha, a client from my practice. When Tanisha became overwhelmed by sadness or anger as a child, her parents would immediately dismiss her, coldly telling her to "get over it" and that she was "too sensitive." Eventually, whenever she felt hurt, lonely, overwhelmed, or full of self-doubt, she learned to tell herself the same things: "What's wrong with you?" and "Get over it, no one cares!" and "Why can't you be cool and keep your feelings together like everyone else?" By the time she was an adult, Tanisha had layers of unaddressed negative emotions that came out in the form of crushing panic attacks.

We can't eliminate anger and sadness, but we can control how open and kind we are to ourselves when we experience these feelings. The next strategies are designed to help you let go of judgment and allow your feelings to surface.

By changing your anger associations, or judgments, you can be at ease with the emotion. Take a moment to consider what you associate with anger—whether memories from your childhood and/or adult experiences.

Write down in your notebook four or five specific words you associate with anger. Do you understand why you associate these words with anger? Where did the judgments come from? Were they ideas you got from observing others or things you were told when you experienced anger? Are your associations with anger mostly negative? If so, why?

Which word holds the strongest association with anger for you? Now, reflect on its opposite. *Can you think of ways this opposite word might be associated with anger, too?*

For example, for many, anger brings up words such as "out of control" and "destructive." Opposites of this include "constructive" or "useful." Expressing anger is *constructive* and *useful* when done in a respectful way that allows us to set boundaries and take care of ourselves.

STRATEGY: JUDGING SADNESS

Sadness is a feeling that comes about due to grief, rejection, feeling defeated, unwanted, or unloved. Typically, each of these instances brings on a sense of loss. The longer the sadness goes unaddressed, the more and more anxious you become.

Whatever the loss may be, it's always okay to acknowledge your sadness about having missed out on something or losing something very dear.

Bring to mind three or four specific occasions when you pushed away the feeling of loss, grief, failure, or rejection.

- Were you honest with yourself or with others about how sad you really felt?

- Instead of feeling your sadness, did you go into an anxiety spiral?

- What stopped you from allowing yourself to be purely sad?

- What kind of judgments might you have been making about your sadness?

- Did avoiding the sadness help or hurt you in the long run?

Letting Go of Judgment
(short meditation)

It's important that you practice observing your emotions without having to immediately push them away. Use this short meditation to gain perspective and space from your moment-to-moment, ever-changing emotions.

Sit quietly and comfortably. Close your eyes. Bring your breath to your conscious attention by noticing your chest rising and falling. Meet whatever emotion or feeling arises in your mind with your inner observer.

Your inner observer carries no judgment. Your inner observer places no pressure on you to act on your emotions. It merely notes what you are experiencing.

For example, your inner observer might verbally label: "chest tight," "anxious," "worried," or "calm," and "at ease." If your inner observer becomes aware of your mind making judgments, simply label it "judging" or "thinking." Notice how when you observe and label, the feeling state passes and then you observe and label the next feeling state.

Nothing you observe is right or wrong. Your emotional experience needs your calm, accepting awareness, nothing more and nothing less.

Turning Toward
Difficult Emotions

Our culture floods us with the message that happiness and success depend on never experiencing suffering or painful emotions. Of course, we all feel negative emotions at times, and when we do, we're left feeling defeated. Feeling that we must have made a terrible mistake somewhere along the way (why else would we be feeling so bad?), we spin our wheels doing whatever we believe necessary to avoid, push away, or somehow "fix" the upset.

We all experience negative emotions, including anxiety. No one is immune. Even people without full-on anxiety disorders go through anxious spikes; it's just part of life. Bringing acceptance to your emotional world means giving up the fight against suffering and pain, so you may be free in spite of it. And, too, it means recognizing and believing that experiencing negative emotions is normal.

Accepting situations and experiences doesn't mean you want them or that you're resigning yourself to a lifetime of emotional pain. Acceptance doesn't mean feeling you're the victim of your pain and that your pain controls you. Acceptance doesn't mean you necessarily like what you're experiencing. Acceptance is the idea: "It is what it is."

The metaphor of the Chinese finger trap used in acceptance and commitment therapy clearly shows how struggling against the experience of difficult emotions only increases negative emotion. The Chinese finger trap is a small woven cylinder that children often enjoy. You place a finger in each end of the cylinder, pull, and—wham—suddenly and unexpectedly your fingers are trapped. Trying to become unstuck, the inexperienced immediately attempt to pull their fingers out. The harder they pull, the tighter the tube becomes, evoking fear and even a little panic. The solution: Push the fingers toward the center of the tube. The tube becomes slightly bigger and then it is easy to wiggle the fingers out.

When we continually push away and avoid our experiences, we become increasingly afraid of the negative. Over time, we stop knowing our feelings altogether. Even pleasant experiences like joy become blocked. We are no longer present but instead live in a survival state, waiting for the next shoe to drop. This crisis-state existence leaves us with an emotional blind spot. After all, if you're completely focused on bailing water out of a sinking boat, you might not notice the life preserver at your side. In my case, spending time processing and ultimately accepting my genetic cancer risk as a reality led to the decision to undergo an elective mastectomy with reconstruction—a literal life preserver that I was unable to see or even consider until I accepted my situation as it was.

Our emotions provide valuable information and guidance. They tell us what we want out of life, what we don't want, how we feel about the people we are close to, and what we need to work on within ourselves. Acceptance allows us to play the game of life with the full deck of cards.

Go Deeper

Understanding
What We Learned Early On

Most of us learn how to cope with our feelings while growing up. We model ourselves based on what our parents did, what they told us about how to handle negative feelings, or how they interacted with us when we were upset. These messages can play out over a lifetime and go unchallenged. For example, Juan, a client I worked with, came to see that whenever he was upset his parents told him he was fine and not to worry. Although well meant, this only increased his upset because he had no outlet to talk through what was bothering him so he could problem solve the situation and find true relief.

Take some time to think through what may be helpful or unhelpful in what you learned growing up about managing your emotions. In your notebook, write about any or all of these prompts that resonate with you.

- Did your caregivers express emotions? Did they cry or get angry? Or did they seem to have a tight lid on their emotions and rarely expressed frustration or sadness?

- Do you think you need to appear in control of emotions all of the time or do you feel completely out of control and so try to clamp down as much as possible?

- Can you recall any expressions from caregivers, coaches, or teachers telling you that you are "too sensitive," "overly needy," or "too emotional"?

- Did your family or caregivers describe you as being very independent/mature as a child? Did you hear a constant "good girl" or "good boy"? Did you feel as if you couldn't be a kid with them? Did you feel there was limited space for you to be you emotionally?

- Consider your memories of joy and happiness in your household as you grew up. Do you recall your caregivers laughing among themselves? Did they notice and label your happiness? Or was joy squelched?

- When upsetting things happened to you as a child, did you feel as if you could talk to your parents openly? Or did you feel your caregivers would judge your upset or overly pressure you to "fix it" in some way? Did you not confide in them at all?

Identify the link between the type of emotional support you were given in childhood and how accepting you are now of your emotional experiences. Start changing the way you support yourself emotionally so you can be more unconditionally accepting of whatever you feel.

STRATEGY: PRACTICING ACCEPTANCE

Although it can be hard to accept painful emotions—to not avoid or push them away—the consequences that come from *not* doing so far outweigh the pain of facing whatever it is you're really feeling. Come up with several examples in your life where your lack of acceptance of your feelings has only caused you more negative emotion or wheel spinning.

As you reflect on these examples, be honest with yourself and acknowledge the #1 feeling you tend to avoid that brings the most consequences to you—sadness, anger, anxiety, guilt, shame, frustration, joy.

Consider the results of avoiding this emotion. Has it increased your anxiety? Caused you to siphon off large amounts of emotional energy in vain? Or has avoiding this emotion blocked joy and contentment?

STRATEGY: SITTING WITH DIFFICULT EMOTIONS

It is likely you have avoided negative emotions because you're afraid of feeling them or you don't know how to feel them. Here is a way to do just that, and it takes only 10 minutes:

1. Set a timer for 10 minutes. Bring to your conscious awareness an emotion you tend to avoid or suppress. Try to conjure it up so you can feel it right now.

2. Observe where in your body you experience the upset or discomfort. Recognize how it feels. See if you can literally visualize the feeling as you experience it in your body. Instead of fighting the feeling, welcome it in.

3. Whisper out loud, "Welcome, I'm glad you're here." See if you can observe the feeling, almost as if you are looking down on a physical thing separate from yourself.

4. Internally note: "I notice a feeling of _____ coming over me." Tell yourself, "I am making room for you," or "I can feel this feeling and also be okay."

5. Notice the anxiety that drifts over you as you allow yourself to face a feeling you always avoid. It's okay to feel this anxiety. It makes sense because you're afraid of this emotion and I'm asking you to feel it. You can be afraid and still invite the emotion in. Show yourself you can enter into the feeling and still be okay.

When your time is up, move forward and let go of this experience.

WRAP-UP

- All emotions are a normal (and helpful) part of human experience.

- Pushing away negative feelings increases anxious thinking.

- Regularly identifying your feelings will decrease anxiety.

- Expressing your feelings will decrease anxiety.

- Accepting your emotional world will decrease anxiety.

- You can experience negative feelings and still be okay.

CHAPTER THREE

Your Body & Physical Sensations

Anxiety and the Body

Cole struggled with debilitating physical symptoms including lack of appetite, racing heart, an inability to concentrate, feeling internally keyed up, and insomnia with racing thoughts. These distressing symptoms were all he could talk about because they were so unnerving. Cole understandably felt as if his body was betraying him and that no amount of anxiety-reduction work would solve this.

Anxiety regularly shows itself with physical symptoms. At some point, sometimes after years of experiencing such symptoms, the dam breaks and the body will no longer be ignored. For Cole this meant such intense heart palpitations that he would become dizzy and pass out. Other people might react in a different way, like succumbing to acute exhaustion, or no longer being able to drive because of severe back spasms, or being unable to concentrate because of persistent headaches. For symptoms like this, anxiety treatment begins once medical causes are ruled out.

When I see clients like Cole in my psychology practice, they are usually surprised that "all" they have is anxiety. For example, for a long time Cole believed that eventually a specific physical ailment would be identified as the root of his very real suffering.

Anxiety impacts the brain and the brain impacts anxiety. In other words, emotions influence our physical functioning and our physical functioning influences our emotional states. Improving our overall physical functioning and body awareness can make all the difference. Cole eventually became more at ease by learning to observe his physical sensations and taking better physical care of himself.

STRATEGY: BODY SCAN

Anxiety inhabits your body. The trick is to start tuning in so you can more quickly recognize the physical signals. The goal of this exercise is to develop awareness for where you carry your anxiety.

1. Pick a position or posture that is most comfortable for you—lying down or sitting up, eyes open or closed. As you do this, let go of judgment. You are simply observing yourself in the here and now.

2. Each time you breathe out, feel your body relax as it releases tension. Recognize when your attention shifts and gently direct it back to your body awareness.

3. One by one, focus on each segment of your body, opening up to whatever is present in that moment. Name the body part and imagine you are breathing into it. Observe areas of tension, strain, pain, or ease: Head . . . Neck . . . Shoulders . . . Arms . . . Hands . . . Chest . . . Back . . . Stomach . . . Thighs . . . Calves . . . Feet . . .

As you come out of this exercise, make a mental note of where anxiety tends to rest in your body so you can tune in to that spot more quickly.

STRATEGY: PROGRESSIVE MUSCLE RELAXATION

When you notice a spike in anxiety and your body feels tense, take 5 to 10 minutes for a progressive muscle relaxation. This strategy also helps when you can't sleep at night or to downshift into relaxation before bed.

Lie down or sit comfortably. In turn, tense each muscle in your body (face, shoulders, hands, arms, stomach, buttocks, legs, feet) while breathing in for a count of 5, and then release the muscle while breathing out for a count of 5. While doing so, pay close attention to the contrast between your experience of muscle tension and muscle relaxation.

Repeat this exercise a few times. Notice your body loosen and gradually become more at ease.

Anxiety's Physical Symptoms

The body's stress system combined with heredity and environmental experiences over time can set the stage for a variety of chronic medical conditions. Persistent exposure to stress through psychological trauma, grief and loss, life transitions, habitual worry, and chronic perfectionism can cripple the adrenal system. The adrenal glands overwork to manage the ongoing stress, and then eventually give way and underwork. The result creates a roller coaster of anxiety spikes followed by exhaustion. Exhaustion can lead to a variety of medical diagnoses.

Anxiety is also linked with the release of stress hormones and chemicals that, over time, can worsen medical conditions. For example, research is showing that stress and chronic pain are likely linked to the same neuronal pathway. Nerve pain increases the expression of the neurotransmitter PACAP, which is the same neurotransmitter the brain releases in reaction to stress. In other words, stress can bring on and/or worsen physical pain symptoms.

The body's biological response to stress can also significantly impact our cardiovascular, digestive, respiratory, and endocrine systems. In a large meta-analysis examining over 20 studies and about 250,000 individuals, researchers found that anxiety was associated with a 26 percent increased risk of coronary heart disease and a 48 percent increased risk of death due to a cardiac-related incident.

The stomach and bowel are directly impacted by the body's fight-or-flight response. Over time, nerves that manage digestion can become reactive, causing unpredictable abdominal discomfort, such as irritable bowel and upset stomach. Although the symptoms are not life threatening, they significantly impact quality of life and can be quite difficult to manage. In addition, people are more vulnerable to stomach ulcers when the stress hormone cortisol is released on a chronic basis.

Anxiety is often present in people with respiratory disease, particularly asthma and Chronic Obstructive Pulmonary Disease (COPD). Fear and worry impact breathing, making these illnesses all the more distressing. The stress reaction due to anxiety is also linked with migraines, rheumatoid arthritis, hyperthyroidism, diabetes, and autoimmune illnesses.

Unfortunately, anxiety is often not considered a significant factor when treating these complicated and often debilitating symptoms. If anxiety is overlooked, medical symptoms may become worse. Knowing which of your symptoms are anxiety related and managing them will improve your overall physical functioning and psychological well-being.

STRATEGY: WHAT STORIES ARE YOU TELLING?

There is a back-and-forth interplay between anxiety and medical illness. The story you tell yourself about your medical symptom(s) and how it impacts you physically is the variable we're going to focus on here. Let's begin with an example:

My client Sierra endured uncomfortable bouts of gastroesophageal reflux disease (GERD). The symptoms were so painful that she was frequently distracted from work and family responsibilities, slept upright at night and so slept poorly, and despite medication had a perpetual burning sensation in her chest. By the time Sierra entered therapy, she had seen a number of gastroenterologists without gaining relief. When I talked to her about the relationship between stress, anxiety, and medical conditions, she was exasperated and felt that I was minimizing her genuine physical illness. After some conversation, Sierra softened her view, although she was unable to believe that her GERD symptoms could be helped by anything other than a medical fix.

We persevered. She started practicing mindfulness, changed her diet, and studied the relationship between stress and physical health. Eventually she became aware that her GERD, although very real and painful, often flared after she experienced a stressful event. Armed with this knowledge, she developed stress-reducing strategies to use each time her anxiety was triggered. She still experienced GERD but reported that the intensity of her symptoms halved. As a result, her symptoms had less of an impact on her life.

Your perception of your ability to manage and control your medical condition makes a difference. Managing anxiety and stress better will not take away your medical condition, but it will enhance your quality of life. Reflect on the following statements and say them out loud a number of times. The more you say them, the less you will feel at the mercy of your physical symptoms.

- I believe I have some control over my physical symptoms.

- I believe if my physical symptoms were to improve it would be due in part to anxiety-reduction strategies.

- The way I think about my physical state impacts my symptoms.

- Exercise will likely improve my physical symptoms.

- My current quality of life could improve.

- My medical diagnosis (or physical symptom) is not entirely out of my hands; I must persevere in living a less-anxious life.

- Stress-relieving strategies and taking good care of my physical self will help me feel better physically.

Working to believe these statements will motivate you toward healthy self-care.

What Else Could You Think About?

Obsessive thinking is a way to avoid facing deeper emotions. Perhaps we worry we can't manage the painful emotions, or perhaps we fear they will overwhelm us.

One client, Jack, told me if he did not think about his medical condition so regularly, he would begin to feel a tremendous sense of helplessness and vulnerability. He felt ineffective and powerless if he was not preoccupied with his health. Hyperfocusing on his body and medical care was a way to not feel like a victim; a way to take charge. With his obsessive thinking, Jack felt like he was *doing* something. This was difficult to experience and express, but once Jack understood his real fear, we could productively work on helping him feel less vulnerable. One way we did this was by looking at what he *could* control about his medical diagnosis, and then using acceptance strategies to deal with the rest.

Jack became more self-aware, noticing when his anxiety was triggered. He did more to quickly identify the sources of his anxious thoughts. He practiced mindfulness daily, exercised regularly, ate a healthy diet, and worked on breathing and positive self-talk. The rest he turned over to his medical team and the universe.

Take a few minutes to reflect and journal in your notebook about the following topic:

If you did not fill your conscious mind with thinking about your medical condition or physical symptoms, the causes, the worries, the what-ifs, and fears that go along with it, what would you be thinking about instead?

Explore what you may be avoiding or missing by engaging in your obsessive thinking. Then, see if you can talk yourself through those deeper emotions and find a way to accept them. Remember, acceptance is not submission; it's a way to take different steps to protect yourself than the ones you've already taken.

It's important to know exactly what your medical situation is, otherwise the mind is free to imagine all sorts of alarming scenarios. And appropriate medical intervention is essential. If you have not done so already, consider making an appointment with a medical doctor who considers the whole picture of physical and emotional health. Tell your doctor about your physical symptoms and also your struggle with anxiety. Ask your doctor for a medical physical with blood work as well as a full thyroid panel test.

Thyroid imbalances impact anxiety and need appropriate medication. Also, make sure your doctor checks your vitamin D level. Vitamin D deficiency can impact mood and energy level. After you talk through the results with your doctor, make three columns in your notebook:

1. Your specific medical issue(s)
   Example: High blood pressure

2. How you're going to address it medically
   Example: Take high blood pressure medication

3. How you're going to address it in terms of anxiety intervention
   Example: Become aware of anxiety triggers; practice mindful breathing 15 minutes a day; exercise four days a week; positive self-talk ("Better managing of my anxiety will improve my physical health")

The Mind-Body Connection

I want you to remember the last time you were genuinely frightened. When it happened, you probably experienced an increase in your heart rate, change in your breathing pattern, or became sweaty, shaky, or jittery. These physical symptoms may have then reinforced your original fearful thoughts. The mind and the body constantly communicate. If your mind is filled with a sense of emotional peace, you are much better equipped to handle medical/physical challenges.

The mind-body connection is empowering because your anxiety symptoms will likely improve, or even disappear, simply by taking good, consistent care of yourself. Healthy sleep, exercise, and nutrition habits usually swiftly improve anxiety symptoms.

STRATEGY: SLEEP

Sleep is restorative in all respects: mood, cognitive functioning, energy, and health. Unfortunately, when we're anxious we do not reap these benefits because anxiety typically interferes with sleep. People who struggle with anxiety wake up to intrusive worries during the night, can't fall asleep, or wake up too early.

Creating a nightly sleep routine places cues in the brain. When practiced regularly, the cues remind us that it's time to start unwinding. The key is to follow the routine consistently so you become accustomed to the cues. Eventually, you will need only to start your routine to feel more at ease and even sleepy.

Many expect to go from alert to asleep with no downshift in between. There's a middle gear: relaxation. Here's an example of a good nightly routine that will help you get into a relaxed, sleepy state. Work to develop one of your own or use this one.

One hour before your desired bedtime (ideally the same time each night), start your routine.

- Unplug from technology. Dock your phone, tablet, or computer away from your bedroom.

- Take a warm bath or shower.

- Change into sleep clothes.

- Drink a warm decaffeinated beverage, such as chamomile tea.

- Do a relaxation exercise: meditate through deep breathing, visualize relaxing imagery, practice progressive muscle relaxation.

- Lie down comfortably and read fiction or something light.

- Turn off your lights when you feel sleepy and your eyes start closing.

- When you can't sleep, don't think, "Why can't I sleep?!" Tell yourself, "It's okay if I don't fall asleep, at least I'm resting." If waking up continues, try progressive muscle relaxation with the lights off.

- Don't worry about the time on the clock. The goal is to relax even if you can't sleep.

- Wake up at the same time each morning.

- If you didn't sleep well the night before, *don't* take a nap or go to bed at an earlier time; stick with the same routine.

IMPORTANT NOTE: *Worry often appears at night because we have been so busy during the day we haven't been able to emotionally connect with ourselves so all the things we haven't thought about crash in once the lights are out. To counteract this, set aside 30 minutes each day for what I call "total worry time." Take out your notebook and put all your worries on the page: Consider how you're feeling, what needs to get done, and what worries you about the days or weeks ahead. Then when the lights are out, your brain won't have to remind you of everything you haven't thought about earlier.*

Anxious energy needs a release or it will continue to run amok. Adding regular exercise into your life will pay off. Thirty minutes of aerobic exercise five days a week will lessen your stress, increase your self-esteem, improve your sleep, and improve your physical and emotional functioning. Feeling good about yourself means you're more likely to cope well because you believe in your ability to do so.

Exercise also increases endorphins, the body's natural painkiller, and decreases the stress hormone cortisol. It's worth it! And if 30 minutes feels like too much too quickly, keep in mind that research is showing that even a 20-minute vigorous walk improves cognitive functioning and mood.

Make a realistic exercise goal. Pick something you enjoy doing so you will continue to do it. For example, walk every day for 15 to 20 minutes. Then after two weeks increase the amount of time or increase to a light jog. Be sure to check with your medical doctor that exercise is safe for your physical condition.

Write down now what your exercise goal is—no goal is too small; any physical movement is better than none. However, each time you exercise, your mood will improve and your anxiety will decrease, so consider doing something on a daily basis.

When experiencing acute anxiety, employ the "10-minute remedy." If you're anxious and you vigorously exercise for 10

minutes—a brisk walk, jogging, bouncing on a trampoline,
jumping jacks—your anxiety will decrease almost immediately.
Lifting heavy objects or weights for a short time can also relieve
anxiety and tension. Endorphins are released and you will feel
naturally at ease. It will wear off, but the 10-minute remedy is a
quick hit for anxiety.

STRATEGY: NUTRITION

Start looking at food as not only one of the great plea-
sures in life but also as a natural means to improving
your emotional functioning. The goal is to eat a varied
diet with plenty of fruits and vegetables. Rid your pantry
of all processed foods and sugar. Adding a variety of
nutrients and decreasing sugar helps the body regulate
insulin and hormone levels, which directly impact mood,
anxiety, and energy levels.

A few specific tips about diet and anxiety:

Water: Our body needs water to function, and if it isn't
functioning properly, mood will suffer. Make sure you're
drinking 8 to 10 glasses of water daily. When experiencing an acute bout of anxiety, pour yourself a tall, icy
glass of water. This will quickly change your physiology,
turn the brain's attention to the cold sensation, and
reduce your anxiety.

Caffeine: It's astounding how many people who struggle
with anxiety also drink a lot of caffeinated beverages.

Make no mistake: Caffeine increases anxiety. Decreasing or eliminating caffeine and other stimulants from your diet will immediately lessen the intensity of your anxiety. Consider removing all caffeine from your diet, and if that's too hard, halve it and work down from there.

Nicotine and alcohol: Both nicotine and alcohol have short-term rewarding effects on the brain but increase anxiety in the long term. If you drink or smoke regularly, take a break and see how you feel. For some people this change alone cures their anxiety overload.

Nutrients: If you have any vitamin deficiencies (check with your physician), you may benefit from taking specific supplements, such as vitamin D or a daily multivitamin.

Go Deeper

Goal Setting for Exercise & Sleep (1-Week Program)

In order to make a long-term impact on your anxiety and give yourself an emotional boost, consider centering your goals this week on regular exercise and sleep hygiene.

Think now about how you can fit in 30 minutes of exercise each day this week. It doesn't necessarily have to be at the same time each day but remember: Consistency makes it easier to stick with a routine. Taking care of yourself needs to be a higher priority in your life, so you might have to give something up or put to the side something that's important to you.

Then, each day do aerobic exercise for at least 30 minutes. Jog, speed walk, bike, hike, play a vigorous sport (soccer, basketball, tag with your kids), take an exercise class. Force yourself to do some kind of activity every day no matter what else is going on in your life. Even when you don't want to do it, remind yourself little in life pays off as much as an investment in exercise. You will improve your physical health, your emotional health, and probably live a longer more fulfilled life—simply by dedicating 30 minutes each day. Bonus: The release of endorphins and other rewarding hormones will help you feel good about yourself.

As we've seen, good sleep hygiene is perhaps the most impactful way to improve mood and anxiety. A regular nightly wind-down ritual cues the brain to calm and switch into sleep mode. Make that a goal, starting with a regular bedtime. Identify which sleep aid techniques discussed previously you will incorporate into your wind-down habit. It's essential to do the routine consistently and at roughly the same time each night.

After a week, journal about how you feel physically and emotionally compared to last week. Do you feel any more positive about your ability to cope? Have you experienced even slightly less physical tension/anxiety this week? Could you continue this for another week?

Everyday Body Awareness

When we're anxious, one worried thought replaces another and another. This can keep us so stuck that even a few moments away from anxiety feels impossible, but it is possible to short-circuit anxious thinking by shifting our attention to our physical sensations.

Try this: Imagine looking at the sky and focusing intently on one small black cloud. Now pull back your perspective so you take in the entire sky, horizon to horizon. From that perspective, the black cloud loses its significance. In the same way, switching your attention from your anxious thoughts to the physical sensations created by those thoughts can alter your perspective.

When you experience an anxious-thought spiral, observe your physical sensations—tight chest, tense shoulders, racing heartbeat, whatever they are—and give them your full attention, breathing in and out. As you acknowledge it ("I see you" or "There you are"), it will likely change to a different sensation. Recognize these sensations are communicating how alive you are in this moment.

STRATEGY: MINDFUL MOVEMENT

Use the simple act of mindful walking to ground yourself into the here and now and to let go of or decrease the intensity of obsessive thinking. You can do this anywhere and at any time—walking to your car, walking around the grocery store, walking around your neighbor-hood, or walking to work.

While walking, focus less on your thinking self and more on your physical experience. For example, what does your foot feel like as you lift it and lower it to the ground? How do your arms feel as you move?

Try to feel the earth from within your body. What is that sensation like? Does the sole of your foot on the ground feel heavy? Can you make it soft?

Explore each of your senses. Notice what you feel on your skin; is the air hot or cool? Do you smell anything as you inhale and exhale?

Simply observe any sounds you hear. Notice what you see. You are here in this moment; feel your presence and your alert state of mind.

With each step, mindfully breathe in, and breathe out. Count your steps as you inhale and as you exhale. How many steps does it take as you inhale? How many as you exhale? Keep your attention on the steps and your breathing.

Each time you become aware of your mind drifting, gently bring your attention back to observing what it feels like in your body to walk. There is no rush; all that matters in this moment is to be aware of your body as it glides through space.

WRAP-UP

- Anxiety impacts the body and the body impacts anxiety.

- Learn to identify and observe (without judgment) where anxiety manifests in your body.

- Anxiety is associated with a variety of medical conditions.

- Healthy sleep, nutrition, and exercise habits typically improve anxious symptoms.

- Practicing body awareness exercises helps reduce anxious-thinking spirals.

Putting the
Tools to Work

*Your intention is set. Anxiety will no longer rule
your life. Now you know it's within your reach
to experience a peaceful emotional life and to feel
physically at ease. The techniques you're learning in this book can reduce anxiety on the spot,
in the moment that it arises. Repeated use of the
strategies will give you consistent, sustainable
symptom reduction. Here's how to start taking
the techniques to the next level through building
longer-term habits and goals.*

From Strategies to Habits

The great pioneering neuropsychologist Donald Hebb observed, "neurons that fire together wire together." Whether it be learning a new language or responding to an abusive parent, repeated experiences over time trigger the same patterns of neuronal activity. At some point, only a tiny cue will trigger that pattern of activity, and you can expect the same events to occur that have always occurred in the past. For example, when you see a red circle in the distance, your brain automatically registers "stop sign ahead." You realize as you approach that it's actually an advertisement on a red circle, but your initial perception told you it would be a stop sign, so you had already started downshifting or easing your foot off the gas. Because old patterns of neuronal activity fire quickly and before we have time to consciously think, changing automatic habits can feel hard.

It takes about 90 days to build a new habit. This is roughly enough time to rewire a bit of your brain. It does take discipline and effort at the beginning, but with practice, the new coping strategies become a natural part of your functioning and routine. Eventually you won't even have to think about what to do to reduce your anxiety. You will automatically have a more peaceful way of being with yourself and coping with the world. This is the payout! To cultivate the ease and calm you want, stick with the strategies and put in steady, consistent effort.

Planning

Take a wide-angle look at how your life is organized so you can begin to think through how and when you will integrate the techniques into your day-to-day routine.

Outside of your responsibilities—work, school, volunteering, childcare, social life, family obligations—what do you do for yourself? When you do have downtime, how do you currently spend it? People with anxiety often feel as if their downtime is unpredictable, that they are at the mercy of others, their schedules, or their anxiety. Stop this pattern by looking at the big picture of your life. Look for opportunities where you can deliberately schedule periods of time to work on your anxiety strategies.

Review what you learned in the last two chapters (looking at your notebook can help) and identify which techniques you want to start with. How often? What times or days of the week are best? You don't have to try every technique; start with two or three that particularly resonate with you. Try to do your anxiety work at the same time or times each day. A consistent time gives the brain a cue that will speed the "neurons that fire together wire together" process.

Track Your Progress

Tracking progress works for many things, like losing weight or saving money. And tracking works with anxiety reduction, too. It's essential to long-term progress that you set up a system where you track on a daily basis the strategies you're using, and the intensity of your anxiety. Here's an example of a quick and easy way to track progress. Each day, check any and all strategies you use from chapters 2 and 3. Also be sure to rate your

STRATEGY	MON
How Do You Feel Right Now?	
Express Yourself	
Exploring Anger	✓
Exploring Sadness	
Judging Anger	
Judging Sadness	
Let Go of Judgment (Meditation)	
Practice Acceptance	
Sitting with Difficult Emotions (Meditation)	
Body Scan	
Progressive Muscle Relaxation	
What Stories Are You Telling?	
Take Care of Medical Health	
Practice Good Sleep Hygiene	
Exercise	
Nutrition	
Mindful Movement (Walking Meditation)	
Rate Your Anxiety 1 to 10 Scale	6

anxiety for the day, using a 1 to 10 scale, with 1 being entirely relaxed and 10 being full anxiety meltdown. For example, you could create a table like this:

TUES	WEDS	THURS	FRI	SAT	SUN
			✓		
		✓			
				✓	
✓					
	✓				
					✓
7	2	5	3	5	8

The 1 to 10 scale is a way to look back and see your progress. At first you may have quite a few 8s or even 10s, but ideally over the course of a month you are going to have more days with 5s or even 4s.

Goal Setting

One way we sabotage our goals is by telling ourselves that we don't have the time it takes to make a change. If you're reading this book, you spend time worried and anxious, yet you don't spend quality time making the changes that will nurture your mental health. Take a moment now to make a goal to tackle your anxiety by doing anxiety strategies on a daily/weekly basis.

You may feel vulnerable acknowledging to yourself, and the people close to you, that you want to improve your anxiety and that you are going to take deliberate steps to do so. You might worry that you won't be successful. It's sometimes easier, particularly in the beginning, to say, "I can't do it," or "I don't need this." If you hear yourself saying these things, it might be because you're afraid of failure. If so, dig deep; believe in your ability to change. You can and will find relief from anxiety, provided you learn to believe in yourself.

When it comes to your anxiety, you likely try to deal with it all on your own. This is hard. Try expressing yourself; tell trusted friends or family and get their support. Sharing a bit about your struggle and how you're working on getting better will make your goal more real and increase your likelihood of success. And it will boost your ability to believe in yourself. Joining an anxiety support group in your community or meeting with a therapist will also help keep you on task.

Another way people self-sabotage is by asking too much of themselves too soon. Start with smaller goals and build from there. Even a little bit of something different creates the scaffolding for more and more growth. Your belief in your ability and your motivation to improve will strengthen each time you are successful and each time you check off implementing a strategy on your calendar.

STRATEGY OF THE DAY

Pick a strategy from this section that resonated with you, and work that strategy into your schedule on a daily basis this week. Helpful daily strategies include practicing acceptance, letting go of judgment, and/or mindful breathing. Before you implement the strategy, visualize yourself doing it. For example, visualize yourself getting up a little earlier and practicing mindful breathing for 10 minutes. After visualizing, practice the strategy in real time each morning.

Pick another strategy that you can work into your calendar at least three times this week. This does not need to take a long time; choose one reasonably achievable for you. For example, this week, commit to brisk walking or light jogging for 20 minutes three times, or schedule a full medical physical with your doctor, or complete the "What Stories Are You Telling?" strategy (page 46).

Go
Deeper

Create Your Weekly "Anti-Anxiety Calendar"

Purchase a weekly or monthly planner or use your digital calendar on your tablet or phone. Then look over the current month. If you have not already done so, write in any work, social, and family commitments and appointments.

Habit formation comes faster when we teach our brains the behaviors we're trying to cultivate on a daily basis. Write in one strategy from the chapters in this section that you're willing to employ every day of the next month.

Now think about when your anxious moments might be during the coming month. Are there specific days of the week or times of the day that you anticipate being particularly anxious? Or are there specific commitments that always trigger your anxiety?

Get ahead of your anxiety by identifying strategies to use before you encounter anxiety-provoking situations, and write down a strategy that you think will be particularly suited for that specific trigger. For example, if you're going to have a pressure-filled meeting at work, you might write on your calendar "express your feelings through writing" when you get home that evening. Or if you're anticipating being annoyed with a friend or family member, you might practice "exploring anger" before the visit so you'll be more aware of and better able to manage your irritation.

Check-In

It's all too easy for the brain to slip back into old habitual patterns. One extremely effective way to prevent backsliding is to make a regular practice of checking in with yourself and consider the ways you're improving/changing.

When you check in, you can assess what's going well and what you might have lost sight of on your path to a peaceful life. And you can recommit to persevering. Rewiring the brain takes practice and time.

How Did You Do?

Start by reflecting on how you're doing every couple of days. Then, as you notice your symptoms improving, check in once a week and then eventually monthly.

- How successful were you with your daily goals?

- How about your weekly goals?

- Based on the 1 to 10 scale, are you noticing any symptom improvement?

Improvement may be subtle at first, but any reduction in the intensity of your anxiety, even going from an 8 to a 7, is an improvement. If you weren't as successful as you'd like, try things differently. Look for other ways to fit in the strategies and be honest about what is blocking you from making more progress. Remind yourself that you want this, and you can and will do it.

STICKING WITH IT

Whatever you do, please, please be sure to recognize and celebrate your successes. I have worked with many people who make major progress, but once the progress is made they minimize or dismiss it. When that happens, they self-defeat future progress.

For example, Hannah started therapy not being able to get a moment's respite from panic, feeling on edge, and muscle tension. She was so consumed by her constant worries that she could not be present, let alone enjoy her life. She made the decision to take charge and became gradually more at ease emotionally and physically. Hannah integrated various techniques into her daily routine and her symptoms improved. She started working again, enjoying sporting events, and spending time with friends.

Sometimes she would have a reoccurrence of panic and find herself in a familiar trance where her entire focus was riveted to worries piling up. It also threw her into a self-critical spiral. Suddenly thinking she had made no progress at all, she would abandon the strategies that had brought her relief.

Progress is not a straight line. Setbacks are part of any growth and change process. Anyone who has raised a child can recall a baby finally sleeping through the night for a few solid weeks. You think those sleepless nights are behind you, then, ugh, the baby starts waking again.

Nevertheless, the typical pattern is for setbacks to become fewer and fewer over time. Eventually the new behavior becomes routine.

Every couple of weeks, reflect on where you started. Remind yourself of what your life was like then and how that anxious life motivated you to adopt a program to improve. Freedom from anxiety is here for you. Open up to the ease and calm that is within your reach. You are worth the investment.

behavior

What You'll Learn
in This Section

Imagine again the triangle with "Feelings" written in one corner, "Behavior" in another, and "Thoughts" in the third. Any change in one corner of the triangle will impact the other two. That insight is at the core of all the strategies in this book. In this section, we are going to focus on your anxious behaviors and how we can change them. Anxiety generally results in two main behavior patterns: avoidance and escape. These two patterns of behavior allow us to limit, or even totally eliminate, our contact with whatever makes us feel anxious. Reducing contact with anxiety triggers makes us feel better temporarily. But avoidance and escape patterns come with hidden costs; one of the most serious costs is that they actually increase anxiety over time.

This section is designed to help reduce your anxiety-driven behaviors. Because of the interconnectedness of those three points on the triangle, this will, in turn, also help reduce anxious thoughts and feelings. For example, if you commit to taking the elevator every day even when your anxiety tells you to avoid it, you will change your thoughts ("Hey, elevators aren't so scary after all") and your feelings (over time, you won't experience as much fear when you take an elevator).

Responding to anxiety with avoidance/escape behavior makes your world smaller and smaller. Eventually you may lose tolerance for even day-to-day, basic interactions. As we explore strategies to tackle avoidance/escape behavior, we'll focus on specific self-defeating habits, doing what you fear, accepting anxiety, and increasing your tolerance for uncertainty.

CHAPTER FIVE

Avoidance & Escape

The Avoidance Paradox

Imagine standing in front of a beautiful pool on a sunny day. The pool is full of swimmers making the most of the sunshine. You're in your suit and poised on the edge of the water, looking as if you are ready to dive in and join them. But in reality, you're frozen with indecision. Yes, part of you wants to jump in. You want to make the most of life and enjoy connection with others. At the same time, a big part of you dreads the shock of the ice-cold water. You're stuck. You see others enjoying the pool, laughing and frolicking freely. You, however, stand on the side. You feel alone. You feel different. You pace. You sit down. You start to imagine people are staring at you, and your anxiety increases. You go back and forth in your head: "Should I jump in? Or not?" You nurture your initial impulse to avoid the cold water with more avoidance. As a result, your fear grows stronger.

Finally, you decide to sit out the pool experience. You feel instant relief, but feelings of self-consciousness and isolation soon arise. Your decision to avoid limits your enjoyment, your spontaneity, and your social life, because your fear has taken control.

The swimming pool is a simple example, but there are many ways we avoid what we fear: We avoid by indecision, by not showing up, by not following through on commitments, by distracting ourselves with meaningless activities, by making excuses and rationalizations.

No longer avoiding what you fear means paying attention to how you feel, not just at the moment you avoid, but over the longer term. Sure, avoidance brings a temporary reprieve—"I'm dreading facing my boss today . . . ah, I'm going to call in sick . . . what a relief to not have to deal with that jerk!" The temporary relief reinforces the tendency to avoid. But the reprieve is almost always short-lived. New anxiety creeps in and takes over. What felt like the sweet taste of freedom becomes bitter with self-critical thoughts about the consequences your avoidance may bring. What will your boss think of you for not showing up? What if you get fired? How will you pay your bills? Are your colleagues criticizing you for not coming in?

Far from relaxing and enjoying a day off, you're spinning back and forth in your mind. Eventually all that anxiety keeps you stuck in avoidance; you don't go to work not only that day, but also the next day and perhaps even the next. Now you likely have actual negative consequences to face.

Avoidance feels protective in the short term, but in the longer term generates real peril and more anxiety than ever. It's worth keeping in mind that the fundamental problem is not the anxiety, but how you respond to it.

Hardwired to Avoid

The fight-or-flight response is produced by an area of the brain often called the "reptilian brain" due to its primitive nature. The reptilian brain evolved very early and relies on an unsophisticated operating system; within milliseconds we flee (avoid/escape) a perceived threat or freeze in place, before we even process the apparent danger. From an evolutionary perspective, this instant all-or-nothing response is effective because, after all, we don't want to waste precious time on details when we encounter a real physical threat.

On the other hand, the reptilian response doesn't work so well at helping us figure out how to address problems that provoke anxiety but are *not actually threatening*. And in modern life, that describes most of the problems we encounter. Even a genuinely scary situation—like a performance review with a boss you don't like—isn't an immediate threat to you. But your reptilian brain doesn't know this, and may react to your fear with a fight-or-flight response that's unhelpful in a professional setting.

In other words, the fight-or-flight response can be triggered even when real danger doesn't lurk. Once the information regarding the perception of danger makes its way to our more evolved "upstairs brain," we're able to rationally determine what level of risk the threat truly poses, as well as problem solve and act strategically. But we have to give that information a chance to get there, without getting stuck in the response generated by our reptilian brain.

When Avoidance Becomes the Problem

Ask yourself if you reflexively avoid or overreact to things that pose no real danger to you. Things that, had you paused and considered more carefully, you might have realized weren't actually such a big deal.

By avoiding the things or situations that trigger you, you're essentially deciding that they are too much for you to manage, when in reality you could deal with them. This diminishing ability to believe in yourself only increases future avoidance. Among other misleading thoughts, your anxious mind probably seriously underestimates your capabilities (more on this in chapter 8). Let's look at how to start changing your tendency to avoid.

As we've seen, avoidance and escape only beget more avoidance. The avoidance loop continues because it's a habit that becomes unconscious. A helpful step is to consciously identify what you're avoiding so you are no longer doing it on autopilot.

Take a moment to reflect on your patterns of avoidance. What do you avoid that only causes you problems in the long run? Here are clues that suggest you're ducking something that matters or has meaning to you:

- Saying you will do something but then not following through.

- Procrastination: delaying a task until tomorrow . . . then the next day . . . and the next.

- Making rationalizations, justifications, and excuses for why you can't do something. ("My alarm clock didn't wake me up.")

- Wasting energy/time on trivial thoughts, tasks, and interactions as a way to distract you from what you should or need to be doing.

- Frequently telling others, or yourself, that you don't feel well physically and that's why you can't do something.

Make a list in your notebook of what you avoid. Keep this focus top of mind, and see if you can catch yourself in the moment you're making the decision to avoid. Then try to make a different choice!

Even dysfunctional, self-defeating behavior continues, or increases, when it's rewarded. People keep smoking because of the rewarding effect of the dopamine hit. Without a serious desire to make a change, this behavior continues in spite of the toll smoking takes on health and longevity.

It's important to identify what is reinforcing, or strengthening, your tendency to avoid even though you would like to stop this behavior.

- What do you *gain* each time you avoid the situations you listed in your notebook? Some people report feeling a sense of lightness, like they dodged a bullet, played hooky, or got out of something truly awful.

- Do you celebrate the reprieve as if you won a prize or accomplished something? Who's really winning?

- Consider if avoidance is reinforced because it means you never have to fully put yourself out there and risk rejection, disapproval, or failure.

- How else might your avoidance be reinforced?

Go Deeper

What is Avoidance Gaining You?

Avoidance is a short-term fix that causes more and more anxiety in the long term. Try this writing exercise to inspire motivation and focus on longer-term, consistent relief, versus quick fixes that never last and have negative consequences.

Write down two lists in your notebook:

1. All the benefits of avoidance. Be very honest with yourself here; no one else is reading this list. Write down why you avoid and the positive feelings that come when you do. Try to emotionally connect with the feelings—for example, the relief of pressure or the power of managing to get out of something.

2. All the benefits of NOT avoiding. How would you feel about yourself—improved self-esteem, proud, less shame, strong? What goal might you gain—greater joy, increased productivity, closer friendships, increased work competence, increased spontaneity?

Now compare the two lists. Which list has more in it for you for the long term? Which list makes you feel better beyond the moment and also helps you achieve broader goals for yourself? Set your intention now on what you want going forward.

Right on Target

Behaviors that you want to reduce or change—like problematic avoidance—are what psychologists call "target behaviors." They are the behaviors that we will target with our interventions. Target behaviors are often unproductive things you continue to do, even though they're self-defeating.

For example, Jase feared public speaking and, as a result, avoided any kind of group meeting at work. In reality, he knew his job well and wished he could show off his talents through public speaking. To start, we targeted Jase's pattern of skipping meetings. We wanted to reduce, and ultimately eliminate, that avoidance behavior. He agreed to at least attend work meetings but not put any initial pressure on himself to speak. Then he built up to gradually asking a question, and eventually making longer and longer statements/comments to the group.

Another client, Alisha, obsessively worried that her boyfriend would break up with her. To prevent these feelings, she sought out constant reassurance from him that he would always be there for her. Like a drug, she needed another and then another hit of reassurance. She wanted to feel safe and secure in the relationship. So we targeted her tendency to seek reassurance. She agreed to reduce requests for reassurance by 25 percent and committed to simply riding out any resulting anxiety spike. In this way she would not have to go cold turkey but could begin to adjust bit by bit. It worked. Alisha started to see that she could manage, and even let go of, her fears for longer and longer periods of time. And it helped Alisha's partner feel less burned out and more compassionate toward her.

Tackling avoidance requires pinpointing target behaviors. The table lists a few examples of goals and how to change your behavior to reach them.

GOAL	TARGETED BEHAVIOR CHANGE
Increase social connection/ closeness with people	Initiate social outings; increase eye contact in social situations
Increase capacity for public speaking	Every work meeting, talk for at least three minutes: ask a question, make a comment, or clarify something
Decrease need for reassurance from partner	Learn to tolerate fears of abandonment: positive self-talk, breathing exercises; seek reassurance but decrease it by 25 percent (three times a day instead of four, decrease from there)
Decrease overthinking spiral/ rumination	Build awareness for rumination by breathing and being mindful; talk to people when upset instead of dealing with the difficulty only in your head, on your own
Be present and participate in life	No drug or alcohol use; build awareness of when you're spacing out or daydreaming; ask questions; be an active listener

Based on your goals, identify three or four target behaviors you would like to change because they get in the way of your larger goals.

Rate how hard it will be to work on each of these behaviors. Use a 1 to 10 scale, 1 being not hard at all, and 10 being nearly impossible.

Rate how motivated you are to work on each of these behaviors. Use the same scale.

Start with a behavior that's not going to be too difficult to eliminate but which is causing enough trouble to motivate you to work on it. So, using the 1 to 10 scale, consider behaviors in the 4 to 6 range for difficulty and at or above 5 on the motivation range. Once you make progress on one target behavior, momentum will develop, and you can work on other items as you wish.

The Great Escape

When we avoid, we work behind the scenes to dodge what we dread. We're planning ahead to totally eliminate contact with the trigger. Escape is different; it manifests when we experience an acute anxiety surge in the moment we contact the trigger. We then do whatever we have to in order to get away from it. Imagine what you'd do if you touched an appliance and got a sudden electric shock—you'd jerk your hand away immediately. You didn't manage to avoid the shock but you did escape it, and minimize your contact with the unpleasant feeling.

For example, if you have a phobia of crowded spaces, you may be perfectly fine most of the time living in a bubble that keeps you in your open-space comfort zone. But terror can take over if for whatever reason you miscalculate and suddenly find yourself in a crowded corner at a museum reception. Your heartbeat jumps. Your face flushes. You shake and jitter. You may even think you're going to pass out or have a heart attack. Similar to a fire alarm sounding, these panic symptoms cause you to immediately make some excuse and flee.

As we've seen, an adaptive survival response in a true emergency can, for the person with chronic anxiety, become a self-defeating pattern of avoiding uncomfortable but nonthreatening situations. When that happens, a person may find themselves in total escape mode for situations that are actually benign— shopping malls, movie theaters, driving, parties, family events, work meetings, doctor's appointments, just to name a few. Giving in to panic and fear through escape means no new learning can occur because you never get a chance to discover if what you fear will actually happen.

If a lion is attacking, jump off a high wall, run toward
oncoming traffic, crash through a sliding glass door—do
whatever you must to survive. But only rarely do most
of us encounter truly life-threatening situations. In those
other circumstances, the ones that feel scary but pose
no real threat, you'll get the best outcomes if you rein
in your fight-or-flight response long enough for your
"upstairs brain" to kick in, so you can make an accurate
risk assessment. Here are three quick and easy strategies
for decreasing the physical agitation and arousal—
shortness of breath, increased heart rate, sweating,
shaking—that accompany panic and anxiety:

1. Take slow, deep breaths, feeling your chest rising
   fully. Each time you exhale, make the exhalation
   a little longer than the one before.

2. If you're too keyed up to breathe freely, count
   your breaths. Counting helps distract your brain
   from anxious thoughts. Count 1 when you inhale,
   2 when you exhale, and so forth up to 20. Then
   start again with 1. Repeat this a few times; the
   arousal will start to decrease.

3. If breathing doesn't work, place your hand
   on your heart. Notice the speed. See if you

can slow it down with your breathing. Put all your attention into observing the beat . . . beat . . . beat . . . of your heart.

STRATEGY: DO WHAT YOU FEAR (a.k.a. EXPOSURE)

We reinforce escape behavior by never staying in the feared situation long enough to see if our anxious expectations are accurate. The only way to test your fears is to put yourself in the situation(s) that ordinarily make you want to bolt, and see if your expectations are realistic. Initially this is going to bring discomfort, but in the long run, it will lead to less anxiety and less escape behavior.

1. Get out your notebook and write down situations that typically trigger an urge to escape.
   Example: Driving

2. Next to each situation write what you believe would happen if you stayed in the situation and did not escape.
   Example: "If I keep driving when I have heart palpitations and shortness of breath, I'll freak out and crash the car."

3. Rate how likely you believe each of your listed expectations is to happen on a 1 to 10 scale (1 being not at all and 10 being extremely likely).

4. Now pick a situation from your list that is moderately difficult, not painfully difficult, but challenging enough that you feel the burn. You're going to intentionally put yourself into this situation to see that you can cope better than you imagine.

5. Start with sticking in the situation for a short time and gradually build up from there. Remember to breathe (use the "Rein In Fight-or-Flight" strategy, page 95) during this exercise. You can and will come out on the other side of this fear.

6. Write down your goal. (We'll use the previous example.) Now go and drive the car. Continue driving for 15 minutes after panic symptoms (rapid heartbeat, shallow breathing, feeling shaky) are triggered. Use purposeful breathing to slow down your breathing and heart rate so the "upstairs brain" can tune in and see that you're actually safe.

7. After you have stuck it out, ask yourself the following:

   • Did your expectation happen? ("No.")

   • What is the evidence that it happened or didn't happen? ("I felt my heart beat fast and I had shortness of breath but continued to drive for 15 minutes," or "I did not crash the car.")

   • What did you learn from this experience? ("I can feel anxious in my body and still drive safely.")

Go Deeper

What Would Happen If?

This short writing exercise is a way to shift your focus away from your fear to the positive feelings and strong sense of self that will come as you rely less on escape and more on moving forward in spite of your anxiety or panic.

Write two stories in your notebook:

1. The story of what you expect would happen if you intentionally exposed yourself to something you've been escaping. Call to mind your worst-case scenario—all the difficult thoughts, feelings, or behaviors you imagine would happen if you stuck with something that instinctively you want to move away from. Perhaps you believe you would die, have to leave in an ambulance, lose your mind, throw up, humiliate yourself . . . whatever it is, write it down. Be as specific as possible.

2. The second story is your best-case scenario of what could occur if you didn't use escape to manage your panic. In this story, you effectively cope and manage whatever thoughts, feelings, or behaviors arise. Despite your discomfort you stay. If you pushed through discomfort, what would be the result? How would you feel about yourself then? Imagine feeling good, strong, capable, even proud.

Uncertainty Intolerance

Remember the Magic 8-Ball from childhood? Ask the ball any question you wish, shake it up, and poof! A triangle floating in water delivers an unequivocal answer. If the Magic 8-Ball really worked, we probably wouldn't have anxiety disorders; because it would always tell us what was coming next, we'd never have to experience uncertainty.

Research shows that people who struggle with chronic anxiety and worry have great difficulty dealing with uncertainty—that is, situations with unknown outcomes. Overthinking—about past events or possible future outcomes—is a way to bridge the uncertainty gap. When we don't know what's going to happen, our brain gets busy generating a bunch of hypothetical outcomes to make us feel like we know more than we do. Take the person going to the doctor for their yearly blood work. Before the tests, during the appointment, and up until they receive the results, they imagine and replay the possible negative results. They even consider various treatment plans for potential diagnoses and diseases.

The problem with this kind of worry and rumination is that anxious minds aren't very rational, and tend to generate possible worst-case outcomes that aren't very likely. So, while worrying about bad outcomes may feel soothing in the short term, it's actually making you more and more anxious over time.

This happens because when we can't tolerate uncertainty, we take on more responsibility than is reasonable for a given situation. A kind of superstitious thinking creeps in, telling us that the "work" of worry is somehow keeping us safe from the hypothetical bad things happening. Whether we think about the blood work results every hour of every day or not, the results will be what they are. Curiously, when the results come back indicating all is normal, there is a self-defeating and irrational tendency to believe that all the worrying made the difference. And then the next time uncertainty creeps in, we will be encouraged to worry again to bridge our knowledge gap.

It's as if we are saying, "If I don't worry about this, then it's my fault when the bad stuff happens." Despite the weight of this pressure, we persevere in our worrying, thinking it will get us somewhere when in reality it's only increasing our anxious state of mind. So we check our email again and again to ensure we haven't missed anything. We triple-check that the stove burners are off, or that the doors are locked every time we leave the house. We seek reassurance, asking ourselves and the people around us, "Are you sure you still love me?" "Have I done everything I can?" "Will my child be safe?" "Do they think poorly of me?" "Will I ever find a partner?" "Am I healthy?" "Am I normal?" "Is everything okay??"

Living that way is exhausting, and over time it diminishes quality of life. The idea that we have to worry or remain hypervigilant so bad things won't happen to us is an illusion. Bad things, including suffering and sorrow, are sadly part of life. It's not your job to become certain of the uncertain. The only real control we have is to accept reasonable uncertainty so anxiety doesn't rob us of joy, or of the pleasure of being fully present in this life now.

STRATEGY: MEETING NEW PEOPLE

Before entering a social situation, we can never know with 100 percent accuracy what will happen, how we will feel, or what others may think about us, which is why social situations often involve a lot of uncertainty anxiety. We can get so caught up in fears over possible judgments/criticisms/slights that we become paralyzed at the prospect of hanging out with people.

The more assertive you are, the less likely you are to fear social interaction. This is because when you exchange eye contact, speak out, put down boundaries, share your opinions, people see you and respect you. And, too, speaking up is a way to clear up misconceptions and miscommunications (both of which are inevitable in the social world) so the same distressing social dynamics don't continue to play out for you over and over again.

List in your notebook what your fears are before entering a specific social situation, and next to each fear write out how you could respond and appropriately handle the situation should it occur.

- What rejections could occur?

  Example: "People won't talk to me at all," or "People will look away and it will feel like I'm not even there."

  Response: "I'll volunteer to help the host," or "I'll make the plan and initiate the event, so I'll be an integral factor."

- What criticisms could occur?

  Example: "If I talk about my job, people will think it's boring and that I'm uninteresting."

  Response: "I'll talk a bit about my job but will highlight the positive, smile, and maybe even joke about it," or "I'll vary my conversation to include my job but also my family or a movie I've seen."

- What things matter to you that cannot be predicted in your social interactions that keeps you avoiding?

  Example: "I want to feel like people like me, but I fear they'll avoid me or won't pay any attention to me."

  Response: "I'll make a point to engage people. I'll ask questions, make eye contact, and make them feel I'm interested in what they say so they'll enjoy talking to me."

If possible, role-play with a friend or therapist where they act the part of the critical other and you act the part of being assertive and defending yourself. Or stand in front of a mirror and literally act out the two sides. Get used to hearing yourself clarify thoughts or statements without being defensive. *A good formula for this is starting with something validating followed by a clarifying statement: "I understand what you mean, but actually I don't see it quite the same way as you do."*

After practicing assertiveness, get out in the world and talk to people. You can tolerate the uncertainty of not knowing what people are thinking and still enjoy the social experiences.

STRATEGY: BUILDING UNCERTAINTY TOLERANCE

Learning to tolerate uncertainty, and seeing that it's possible to live with it, is actually much easier in the long run than overthinking possibilities and imagining terrifying outcomes.

Here are four steps toward increasing your tolerance for uncertainty:

1. Instead of avoiding uncertainty, seek it out.

2. When uncertainty presents itself, courageously welcome it with open arms: "I see you, uncertainty, and I can and I will continue to live fully while you're by my side."

3. Reduce behaviors that reinforce your belief that you can't handle uncertainty. If you compulsively check things, check every few days instead of

every day, or every five hours instead of every hour. If you constantly seek reassurance, see if you can self-soothe through positive self-talk, journaling, exercise, deep breathing, before you ask for another dose of reassurance. If you're ruminating about a what-if scenario, internally label it "can't be certain of the uncertain."

4. While strengthening the muscles that will let you manage uncertainty, pay close attention to the parts of your life where you *do* have control. For example, being present and attentive to children is one way we can impact their future happiness. Exercising and eating well helps with health and feeling good. Building communication skills and positive experiences together helps a range of relationships stand the test of time. You may not be able to predict uncertain outcomes, but those are all things you can do to help ensure things will go well in the long run!

WRAP-UP

- Avoidance feels relieving in the moment but in the long run increases anxiety.

- The desire to avoid/escape fearful situations is part of our brain's fight-or-flight response.

- The problem is when fight-or-flight is triggered without an actual threat.

- Challenge your instinct to escape or avoid so new learning may occur.

- Uncertainty in life is unavoidable; accepting this truth decreases anxiety.

CHAPTER SIX

Acceptance & Approach

Making Peace with Anxiety

Anxiety serves an important function. Worry and concern enable us to tune in, connect with others, take care of ourselves, and have empathy. Anxiety also motivates us to set goals, take action, and pay attention to what matters. I sometimes see people in my practice who don't have enough anxiety. That might sound strange, but they come in feeling unmotivated, lost, and without purpose. Chances are, if you live with anxiety, you're fully invested in your life's course. You have the drive needed to achieve an enriching and meaningful life. The key, however, is to not squander your precious energy on a struggle *against* anxiety.

Many of us have a sense that we aren't living a "good" or "happy" or "correct" life if we experience even low levels of distress. If you feel this way, you probably expend a lot of energy trying to prevent the unpreventable. Joy, love, and pleasure are magnificent aspects of life. However, in the small print on life's contract you'll find that hardship, loss, suffering, setbacks, and, yes, anxiety, are also part of the deal.

Instead of trying to rid yourself of things that can't be changed, like distress and discomfort, change your *relationship* with anxiety by accepting it. Give up the futile struggle against your feelings and allow your anxiety to come and go—as feelings always do.

Imagine yourself as a surfer, moving with, not against, your waves of emotion, and accepting those waves as they come. You can't control the waves, but you can take them as they are, which will help you move through life more smoothly.

Accepting anxiety doesn't mean you're a victim of it or that you're giving up and allowing it to control you. Acceptance doesn't even mean you like what you're experiencing. Acceptance is the idea that it is what it is. When you look out the window and see rain you don't say to yourself, "It's raining, I have to fix this!" You also don't say, "I'm a victim of the rain," or "I'm being abused by the rain," or "It's raining, I give up." Perhaps you don't love the rain, but you pull out an umbrella, you keep moving forward, and you know that eventually the rain will stop.

Try this experiment to experience the change in perception and emotional freedom that true acceptance brings.

For this exercise, get your notebook and also find a bandana or light cloth you can use as a blindfold. I want you to write a few sentences while wearing a blindfold about your understanding of the role of acceptance in managing anxiety. You're to write as clearly and legibly as possible, making sure to keep the letters and words lined up, even though you won't be able to see what you're writing. You can do anything you need to help you with this, except remove the blindfold. Do your best to try to figure out a way to write as straight as you can in spite of not being able to see.

Now do the exercise again. This time, don't worry about writing straight and on the lines, or making sure your letters are clear. Just write while wearing the blindfold.

Can you feel the difference? Once you accept the blindfold, you're liberated from the anxiety about it.

STRATEGY: CLARIFY YOUR VALUES

Values are the things in life we cherish most, the things that give our lives meaning. Common examples of core values include family, spirituality, health, and community. Living a life that matches your core values increases self-esteem, joy, and quality of life. The good news is, the strategies you're learning here will help you channel your energy away from anxious patterns and toward the values that matter most to you, in spite of, or alongside, your anxiety symptoms.

A good way to get in touch with your values is to imagine yourself on your deathbed. This can be difficult, but imagining life ending can sometimes connect us with what we want most.

- What do you want others to know and remember about you, that you did or didn't do, during your life?

- How do you want to impact the larger world?

- How do you want others you care about to experience you?

Consider writing down what you value in each area of your life as listed on the next page; remember, a value can be that you don't value that particular area.

Relationships (romantic, friendship, family, parent, child):

Professional:

Education:

Religious/spiritual:

Community:

Hobbies/interests:

Psychological growth:

Physical health:

STRATEGY: COMMITTED ACTION

Identify what you can do *now* to start living the kind of life you truly desire. Any small step toward your values will improve your mood and anxiety. Get out your notebook and map out a plan to start taking committed action toward something you value. Here's how:

1. Identify value:
   Example: Psychological growth

2. Identify goal:
   Example: Increase self-esteem

3. Identify step to take to reach goal:
   Example short-term action: "Every day do one task that makes me feel competent—pay the bills, make a meal, exercise, volunteer, help a friend."

Example long-term action: "Ask boss about what's needed for a promotion," or "Sign up for a class."

4. Now take action!

Go Deeper

Your Best Life

The story you tell yourself about who you are and what you can and can't do influences every aspect of your life. Although you may take your story as fact, it is not. The accumulation of negative experiences over time can give us a sense of ourselves that is entirely false. We are so accustomed to our story that we don't challenge it or recognize the ways it blocks our growth. Your story can be changed.

- Rewrite your story so it can support who you truly want to be.

- In this process, consider which ideals/values you care about and want to cultivate.

- Write about what your best life would look like and also how you would feel on the inside if you were actually living this life.

- Write specific, doable, action items that will move you toward living this life starting now, today.

Do the Scary Thing

For many of us, it's tempting to think the only way to emotional freedom is to eliminate our anxiety entirely. But as we've seen, total anxiety elimination is self-defeating because of anxiety's many benefits and, of course, because it is an impossible task. Feeling anxious from time to time is something to accept, not struggle against.

Accepting you're going to feel anxious at times— sometimes quite anxious—frees up psychic space that was occupied by willing anxiety away. This opening is a portal for achieving goals and living a meaningful life *while anxiety is present*.

In fact, when you make room for anxiety to be present without sounding the fire alarm, you'll find there's value in simply noticing where anxiety crops up. Frequently we become anxious about things because they matter to us. For example, when we worry about a social interaction it's probably because we really value having a social life. If we tremble in the face of a job interview, it's because professional achievement is important to us. We don't usually get anxious about things that are irrelevant to our lives and values.

Instead of turning on yourself when anxiety rears its head, make room for it and for what it can teach you. Accept yourself, wholly and completely, the positive and the negative. Approach what you're afraid of, because whatever is on the other side of that fear matters to you. And that's important, because *you* matter.

Paradoxically, fully accepting anxiety relieves anxiety. To do this, however, you have to legitimately accept it as an inevitable part of your life. Accepting anxiety just so it will "go away" won't work. Tell yourself (*and mean it!*), "My anxiety will forever come and go," and "I can still be okay and live a valuable life with anxiety."

Maybe you've experienced the freedom that comes with true acceptance in other parts of your life:

Just when you accepted you wouldn't find love, you found it.

Just when you accepted your unsatisfactory job situation, it improved.

Just when you accepted a loss, something was gained.

Just when you accepted your flaws (or the flaws of someone else), they stopped upsetting you.

Just when you accepted your diagnosis, you became healthier in other ways.

Acceptance brings less obsessive focus and energy spent on whatever is troubling us. As we become less singularly focused, our lens expands to the larger picture. We have the space to strategize, take risks, and do more to improve our circumstance.

Use this visualization exercise to get in touch with what you might gain if you push through your anxiety.

1. Bring something to mind that matters to you but that you've avoided or neglected because of anxiety and fear. Picture the details. Paint the scene in your mind's eye.

2. Try to conjure what you would feel in your body if you approached what you are afraid of. Notice the physical cues. Can you feel your heart rate increase or your stomach sink? Remind yourself that you're safe; you're just pretending.

3. Imagine you follow through with whatever used to frighten you into inaction, and imagine how you would feel if you did that. What would you gain?

Anxiety Is Not the Boss of You

Ideally, when our anxiety response is triggered, we make a swift assessment of how dangerous the situation at hand really is. Then we're able to either manage the situation appropriately ("Get out of the house, there's a fire!") or self-soothe ("You're okay, take a deep breath."), return to a calmer baseline, and move on. When we experience chronic anxiety, fight-or-flight is triggered so frequently that we are forever on guard for potential threats, and can never truly relax.

Anxiety can be like a tyrant that controls us to such an extent that our true nature fades into the background. Over time it gets harder and harder to recall who we are and what we want, separate from anxiety, or believe there is another way to live. Yet it's possible to break free. You can go your own way, do your own thing; you can be the boss of the anxiety.

Take the example of Mateo, a high school football player I worked with in my psychotherapy practice. A gifted athlete, Mateo was nonetheless consumed by anxiety regarding his performance on the field. Over time this anxiety stopped him from going on the practice field at all, which only increased his anxiety and negative feelings about himself. Not practicing meant his skills weren't improving. Mateo worried recruiters wouldn't see what he could do and all would be lost.

I suggested to him, "You know you're really anxious right now. Your anxiety is telling you to stay home and give up on your dream of getting a football scholarship. You believe you have to do what the anxiety tells you. But you don't have to listen. You're in charge, not the anxiety. You could go to practice *while you feel anxious*."

At first, Mateo, like many of us, remained stuck on the idea that he can't live with anxiety: "But I don't want to feel anxious! I have to figure out the anxiety first." Then he made the connection: "Well, I guess I'm going to feel anxious either way. I didn't go to practice today and I feel even worse than yesterday, but at least if I go to practice I haven't lost anything else."

And that's it. If you make your choices *in spite of anxiety*, you're retaking control of yourself and your actions—you're retaking control of your world. Now you are free. Free to strive to become a college football player, develop close friendships, fall in love, travel, be spontaneous, take the final tests to get the degree, take that medical test that could save your life, speak up in the meeting so your boss will give you that promotion, start a new business, plan a party.

Anxiety will not disappear, but it will no longer be your tyrannical boss—you, your true nature, will be the boss.

STRATEGY: WATCHING YOUR THOUGHTS

Use this mindfulness exercise to better connect with the part of you—the observer—that is separate from your anxious feelings and thoughts.

1. Sit quietly and comfortably. Become an observer of your thoughts and sensations. You're not overwhelmed by your experience and you're not pushing it away or judging it. Your experience just is what it is.

2. Notice that as each thought passes it is replaced by another . . . and another . . . and another. Similar to lying on your back watching clouds and labeling their varying shapes and nuances: "fuzzy cloud," "smoke cloud," "bird-shaped cloud." Watch your thoughts as they come and go and label them: "worried thoughts," "fear thoughts," "planning thoughts," "happy thoughts."

3. Label your observations as they come up using the sentences below. These sentences are ways to separate your observing self from your emotions and thoughts:

- "I am aware I am having the thought that _____."

  Example: I am bad/weak/failure . . .

- "A feeling of _____ has come over me."

  Example: sadness/dread/hurt/sorrow/joy

- "I am experiencing the thought _____."

- "I notice a narrative that tells me _____."

- "I am noticing a sense of _____."

- "I am noticing a body sensation of _____."

STRATEGY: IN VIVO EXPOSURE

In vivo is just a fancy way of saying, "in real life," and for our purposes, it means you need to experience the situations you're avoiding. Anxiety has dictated a number of your choices and caused you to miss out. Calling up your fears in real time, by approaching what you usually avoid, will show you that you can work through your anxiety in the moment and get out on the other side. What's on the other side? A life full of experiences you value. (When you try your first in vivo exposures, find a trusted friend to accompany you so you have support if you start to feel overwhelmed.)

Pick something that you've long avoided because of anxiety. This should be something that will be hard but that you can imagine pushing yourself to do. Examples might be calling a friend or relative, going somewhere, speaking up in a group, asking for something you need, telling someone something you've needed to say for a long time. Take doing the task slowly. Remember, the anxiety will be there as you push forth and that's okay. Here's how:

1. Take action: Do something you avoid and fear that blocks you from gaining something important to you.

2. Rein in fight-or-flight: Bring down physiological arousal by paying attention to your breathing. Make each exhalation longer than the one before.

3. Support yourself: Tell yourself, as you push forward toward your goal and feel that surge of anxiety, "I can and I will push through. I can and I will push through. I can and I will push through . . . "

When we're anxious, we don't focus enough on the relief and even pleasure we experience when we push through the anxiety and get to the other side. Take a moment now to be aware of what good came from exposing yourself to the situation you have previously avoided so you will be sure to do it again.

- Do you feel any relief in your body?

- Do you feel any pleasure or pride in knowing you did the thing?

- Did anything good come from doing it?

- Can you imagine doing it again or something similar?

- Which makes you feel better about yourself, approaching your fears or avoiding/escaping them?

Giving Up the Struggle

It's tempting to live life in a constant state of longing. We long to not experience upsetting or anxious feelings. We long to win. We long to be better. We long to be free of pain and full of pleasure. And we berate ourselves when we don't achieve what we long for. This mind-set can make life an endless race to get something, and then something else, and then something else. Deep down we believe this struggle is one day going to lead to an end to all of our suffering, an end of wanting more, and an end to ever feeling bad.

This belief is a fantasy that encourages anxiety to flourish. Anxiety on some level is never going to end. Believing it can somehow be controlled or erased becomes a barrier that prevents people from improving the quality of their lives here and now.

Take, for example, planning a vacation. You can choose to approach the planning with anxiety, frustration, or aggravation. You might worry that you won't be able to do what you want to do on the trip, that the flights will be horrendous, and that all the planning is taking away time from other things you should be doing. At times you may even tell yourself, "This trip isn't worth all this planning, ugh, I give up!" By the time you take the trip you may be filled with such resentment or annoyance over the planning and packing that nothing about the trip will quite make you happy. You return home dissatisfied and unfulfilled. You vow to take another, better, more perfect trip in the future.

Alternatively, you can accept the planning process— even embrace it. You have to do it anyway, so you might as well enjoy it. You can conjure a feeling of excitement and imagine your future pleasure as you think through what you want to do. You can spend time looking at photos, reading articles, and creating an agenda. When you hit setbacks, you can be flexible and think of other ways to still get much of what you want out of the trip.

Dealing with anxiety is similar, in that there's a choice: On the one hand, you can forfeit the present moment and succumb to anxiety, or even self-criticism for *feeling* anxiety. On the other hand, you can make room for a larger experience of yourself other than as just an anxious person. If you want the latter, when setbacks hit, adjust to the new wave like that agile surfer, or take a turn in a different direction. Do that and anxiety's inevitable presence will not dominate and rob you of the enriching experiences you deserve.

Go
Deeper

Exploring Your Struggle

Take some time to sit down and journal about what your struggle with anxiety is like for you. Here are a few prompts to focus your writing:

- Write about the ways you have attempted to fight anxiety. For example, trying to anticipate fear/self-doubt/worry; making choices in hopes they will keep anxiety at bay; spending time problem-solving about things that can't be solved; trying to make certain the unavoidable uncertainties found in every life.

- Many people blame themselves. Consider the ways you may have been too hard on yourself— judgmental and self-critical—because you feel you "shouldn't" be struggling with anxiety.

- Consider how many parts of days, weeks, and years have been consumed by anxiety. What would it be like to give up this struggle and accept anxiety? What would you do with the gift of that free mental space?

- As you write, see if you can connect with a feeling of compassion for yourself and for what you have endured in your struggle.

This strategy is a way to practice giving up the fight against your emotions. Instead of struggling against them, you're actually going to lean in to whatever emotions you might be experiencing—the pleasant and the unpleasant. Try to actually invite anxiety (and other unpleasant feelings) to come over you.

1. Sit comfortably in a quiet location. When anxiety appears, instead of fighting it ("This is wrong," "Make it stop."), let go of control and give up the struggle. Welcome anxiety in with open arms: "Yes, I see you, anxiety, and there's space for you here with me." Meet the surges of unease or worry with warm acceptance. You can accept your feelings even though they cause you discomfort.

2. You're not attempting to change the feeling, push it away, or keep it present. You're aware of whatever it is, *as it is*. You're letting go of control in favor of awareness.

3. As you experience the anxiety, ask yourself, "What else may be here?" Explore for deeper emotions that may be hiding under your anxiety. Many anxious people have not grieved something from their past or fully acknowledged a hardship they suffered. For example, perhaps you're

anxious about your partner possibly leaving you. Dig deeper; what is this worry connected to from your past? When do you remember first feeling anxiety over someone leaving? Perhaps you trace this feeling to your parents' divorce and your dad moving out. Now invite in that sadness or anger; see if you can notice where you feel it in your body. Stick with the feelings.

4. Work to uncover the root emotion to which each anxiety branch may be attached. Oftentimes, getting at the root, where the emotion first presented, can entirely relieve the anxious feelings. Tell the feelings they're welcomed here with you. Validate them as real and worthy of your attention.

STRATEGY: TAKE YOUR ANXIETY ALONG FOR THE RIDE

If you're like many anxious people, fear and apprehension stop you in your tracks. You feel as if you have to wait for anxiety to go away before you can get on with your life. It's actually the opposite: for your anxiety to diminish, *get on with your life*!

- Take a moment to identify and be aware of your anxiety. Then task yourself with an activity, errand, or outing. This doesn't have to be an all-day event. (You can work up to that.) Even going to the grocery store or running a few errands while in an anxious state will do the trick.

- Make sure you follow through completely. In other words, don't give up once you're at the grocery store or after completing one errand. Remember, you're apt to feel anxious wherever you are, so you might as well get some things accomplished while you're anxious (and it might just help you to be less anxious later).

- Once you complete the task, see if your anxiety decreased at all as a result. Even if it didn't, congratulate yourself that you did what you needed to do in spite of the anxiety. Do it again when you have an opportunity.

WRAP-UP

- Accepting that anxiety will forever come and go is liberating.

- Stopping the struggle against anxiety creates room for an enriching life.

- Identifying your values and larger goals will enhance your quality of life.

- Making choices and taking action on these larger goals in spite of your anxiety is empowering.

- Fully accepting anxiety relieves anxiety.

CHAPTER SEVEN

Putting the Tools to Work

Implementing anxiety techniques on a routine basis means you can start to make choices for yourself that reflect your larger goals and values, in spite of anxiety. *You're no longer only an anxious person; you are a person who, along with anxiety, has a rich and meaningful life. Here are ways to turn the strategies you're learning into consistent habits that will enrich your life for the long term.*

From Strategies to Habits

Repeated use of these techniques in a structured, determined manner will bring you relief far beyond managing your symptoms. Consider the challenging task of quitting smoking. Smokers say it usually takes three months for nicotine withdrawal symptoms to leave the body. Those three months require deliberate effort to adopt a new learning pattern, but the rewards clearly outweigh the effort. Three months is nothing compared to a longer, healthier, and more satisfying life.

Similarly, take the example of Julia. Julia felt extremely anxious driving on highways with congested lanes and higher speed limits. Each time she drove on a highway, the same pattern of neurons fired and a panic attack soon ensued. Julia's mind reeled with imagined bad outcomes. Over time, even the thought of highway driving triggered panic. Eventually she stopped driving on highways altogether.

In the moment, avoiding what makes us anxious feels like the fix. In the long run, the avoidance increases anxiety. With treatment, Julia made a commitment to overcome this anxiety. She began by visualizing herself driving and coping well. She also practiced deep breathing to rein in the fight-or-flight response and supportive self-talk: "I can and I will push through to the other side." At first the old anxiety reaction came flooding back in. She persevered. After two weeks of visualizing, she drove on a highway again. After two months, she was regularly behind the wheel and reported that her anxiety had dropped from 10 to 5 on a scale from 1 to 10.

Julia pushed through. Not only did her symptoms improve but her quality of life also improved. She was now able to spontaneously visit her mom and friends. Most importantly, she felt like the independent and capable woman she always knew herself to be.

Planning

Reconsider when you will integrate the techniques you planned in chapter 4 into your daily routine. If you have already begun to do so, maybe your planning is working. If you have not started to use the strategies regularly, consider whether you've made a realistic plan. For example, if you commit to practicing the various strategies for 20 minutes at the end of the day and you aren't following through, maybe two 10-minute sessions is a better way for you to start.

Be flexible and open to new ways of structuring your life, but do schedule time, ideally a little bit each day, to work on anxiety reduction.

Track Your Progress

It's important to long-term progress that you set up a system whereby you track, ideally on a daily basis, the strategies you're using and the intensity of your anxiety.

On the next page is an example of a quick and easy way to track progress. Each day, check any and all

Continued on page 138

STRATEGY	MON	TUES
What Are You Avoiding?		
Why Are You Avoiding It?		
Identify Targets		✓
Rein in Fight-or-Flight	✓	
Do What You Fear		
Meeting New People		
Building Uncertainty Tolerance		
Acceptance		
Values		
Committed Action		
Imagine a Scenario		
Stop Missing Out!		
Watching Your Thoughts		
In Vivo Exposure		
How Did It Feel?		
Inviting Difficult Emotions		
Take Your Anxiety Along for the Ride		
Rate Your Anxiety 1 to 10 Scale	7	3

	WEDS	THURS	FRI	SAT	SUN
	✓				
					✓
			✓		
		✓			
				✓	
	5	2	3	6	7

strategies you use from chapters 5 and 6. Also be sure to rate your anxiety for the day, using a 1 to 10 scale, with 1 being entirely relaxed and 10 being full anxiety meltdown. For example: The 1 to 10 scale is a way to look back and see your progress. At first you may have quite a few 8s or even 10s, but ideally over the course of a month, you're going to have more days with 5s or even 4s.

Goal Setting

When the rubber meets the road, and you have to actually start implementing your plan, self-doubt will creep in. Self-doubt is the enemy of inspiration and change. It's all too tempting to turn to excuses: "It's too hard," "It will take forever," "This is going to be awful." Allow that to happen and the mental energy required to improve will be tapped out.

You want to be released from your struggle with anxiety, which is why you're reading this page now. However, for many, the idea of change brings on competing feelings. Yes, there is hope for something better but also fear that you can't get there. When doubt looms, remind yourself that *anxiety is highly responsive to treatment*. People who practice these techniques on a regular basis usually improve. The need for effort doesn't mean results won't come, it just means it will require work.

Take this moment to set a couple of goals for yourself based on what you read in chapters 5 and 6. These should be overarching goals that you can come back to repeatedly for motivation to stay the course.

Maybe you recognize all you've missed out on because of avoidance behavior, and you want to stop missing out. Or perhaps you became more clearly aware of what is meaningful and of value in your life, and you set the goal of making space for those values, regardless of your anxiety.

Pick a few strategies from this section that you can incorporate on a daily basis. For example, an excellent daily strategy that is quite grounding is "Watching Your Thoughts" (page 120). Sit quietly even for five minutes and observe your thoughts, similar to watching clouds. Thoughts will arise, and they will pass by—you don't have to respond, you only have to observe them. Or sit quietly and practice acceptance of something troubling you, or invite your anxiety in and accept those feelings and sensations.

Another helpful strategy is "Take Your Anxiety Along for the Ride" (page 128). In this case, you commit to keeping up with tasks and commitments, even when you're in an anxious state. You simply tell the anxiety, "Alright, I know you're there; you're just going to have to come along with me today!"

Pick a few larger strategies that you can work into your routine at least three times this week.

A good place to start and one that will immediately boost your mood and decrease anxiety is to spend some time each week on committed action—this could be spending time with a loved one or volunteering at a local homeless shelter/animal rescue center. Taking practically any action, no matter how small, that matches your values will inspire you and also lessen anxiety, even if only slightly.

Go
Deeper

Create Your
Weekly Strategies Calendar

Revisit the weekly strategies calendar you created in chapter 4 (page 73). Take a moment to look over the current month. If you have not already done so, write in work, social, and family appointments and commitments.

People make great progress by simply committing to using one strategy on a daily basis. This can be a simple/easy strategy, but doing it daily encourages the habit to become gradually more automatic. Write in one strategy from chapters 5 and 6 that you're willing to commit to using every day of the month. When you realize you missed a day(s), which will occasionally happen, just pick up where you left off.

Assess what's coming up by digitally or manually marking red, yellow, and green zones on your calendar. Red zones are those that are more anxiety fueled, green are those where you expect to be fairly at ease and feel less internal pressure, and yellow are in the middle, where you imagine you will feel neither very anxious nor very relaxed.

Take a step back and look at how much of your month is red and how much is green. If there's a predominance of red, you're likely carrying too much dread about your activities, which is no way to live. One of the single best ways to improve mood is to have things to look forward to. Can you reduce the red on your calendar and increase the green? Even a few eliminations can make a noticeable difference.

On days or times where you anticipate anxious triggers, or see a red zone on your calendar, write down a strategy (or strategies) that you think will be particularly suited for that specific trigger. For example, if it's a dreaded social encounter, you might put on your calendar to "practice acceptance," or "practice being assertive in social situations." Or if it's something you want to avoid but need to approach, you might practice "imaginal exposure," where you visualize yourself doing the thing you want to avoid.

Check-In

One of the reasons weekly psychotherapy is so effective for treating anxiety is that the regular meeting serves as a cue for the brain, a reminder of the ultimate goal—a sense of peace and well-being—and the tools needed to get there. You can do this on your own, but do commit to checking in with yourself on a regular basis. Use this time to note your progress and problem solve about what you could tweak or do differently to be even more successful. The key is to be flexible and try things differently if your anxiety is not improving, but don't give up. It takes flexibility and patience, but ease and calm await.

How Did You Do?

Start by reflecting on how you're doing every couple of days. Then as you notice your symptoms improving, check in once a week and then eventually monthly.

- How successful were you with your daily goals?
- How about your weekly goals?
- Based on the 1 to 10 scale, are you noticing any symptom improvement?

Improvement may be subtle at first, but any reduction in the intensity of your anxiety, even going from an 8 to a 7, is an improvement. If you weren't as successful as you'd like, try things differently. Remind yourself that you want this, and you can and will do it.

STICKING WITH IT

It takes practice to integrate new anxiety-reduction routines into your habitual thinking and day-to-day life. Perseverance requires that you do not beat yourself up for setbacks. Any time we make a change or learn something new, we experience disappointments and obstacles. Use setbacks as learning tools, teaching you what to do differently next time. Then start again.

No matter what the moment, the day, or the week is like, the key is to not give up. You can start again at any time. Cultivate patience and compassion for yourself. You are brave to dedicate yourself to changing your life. You will be rewarded for your work!

thoughts

What You'll Learn
in This Section

Once again, call to mind the image of a triangle with "Feelings" in one corner, "Behavior" in another, and "Thoughts" in the third. As we've seen, working in any corner of this triangle will change the other two. In this section, we're going to relieve your anxious, repetitive thought patterns. Anxious thinking means you're frequently flooded by repetitive and intrusive thoughts. You wish you could turn your mind off, but the catastrophic or worried thoughts just keep coming. Feeling mentally on edge in turn fuels anxious feelings and avoidance behaviors.

For example, imagine receiving an invitation to a friend's birthday party. You might immediately think something like, "No one is going to talk to me if I go. I'll feel awkward." If you have that thought often enough, or just believe it enough, you might end up skipping the party, even though you like your friend and don't want to miss out. Or if you do go to the party, your anxious thinking might nag at you the whole time, making it an ordeal instead of the fun experience it should be.

The strategies in this section will help you challenge the kinds of anxious thoughts that interfere with your quality of life. The key thing I hope this chapter teaches you is that you can't believe everything you think. We'll explore why our thoughts often need to be challenged, and you'll learn specific strategies that can be used to do just that.

CHAPTER EIGHT

Thoughts vs. Reality

Don't Believe Everything You Think

You, your resilience, and your capacity for growth are actually much stronger than your anxious thoughts—although it probably doesn't feel like that most of the time. For the anxious mind, a flood of worry can rise in a matter of minutes, sweeping you away to a place where what began as a passing thought becomes in your head an absolute truth. If you watch your thoughts carefully, you will catch yourself jumping to extremes and generalizations.

Imagine you get a ticket for a minor fender bender and then you have the thought, "What if they sue me?" Anxiety quickly evolves that thought into, "They *are* going to sue me!" Or say you get some negative feedback at work and have the thought, "My boss sees problems with my work." Anxiety steps in, and the thought becomes, "I'm going to get fired." Or you realize your mom hasn't returned your phone calls and you wonder why. Anxiety turns wondering into, "She must have had an accident." Or you realize your partner hasn't returned a text all day and you worry, "My partner doesn't care about me anymore," quickly followed by, "He's leaving me!" This pattern of taking one small, worrisome thought to an extreme can also be initiated by a physical sensation: "My heart is beating fast . . . I must be having a heart attack!" There are all sorts of frightening, unlikely places your anxious thoughts will take you—but only if you let them! Believe it or not, you can intervene and slow this process down.

Imagining catastrophes and worst-case scenarios is emotionally draining and keeps us from being fully present in the here and now. But we can learn to sort our thoughts so that things like over-the-top speculations and black-and-white thinking are moved to the "discard" pile, at least until you have solid evidence that those thoughts are realistic. Start sorting helpful from unhelpful thoughts by taking a little time (even if only a few moments) to slow down and become aware of what you're thinking before you react.

When we slow down, we create space to observe our thoughts and see if they're as realistic as they might seem initially. So the thought, "I'm going to get fired" becomes "I'm having the thought that I'm going to get fired." The thought, "My girlfriend is breaking up with me" becomes "I'm having the thought that she's

breaking up with me." Taking a more curious and obser-
vational stance makes room to challenge the accuracy of
your thoughts and weigh their usefulness to you.

This strategy challenges your thoughts in a new way.
The exercise is designed to help you distinguish between
your actual experience and your *interpretation* of what
you're experiencing. When we observe, not overthink,
we become liberated from anxiety.

1. Bring all your attention to your heartbeat. Place
   a hand on your heart. Or see if you can turn your
   awareness inward and actually feel the beating
   within your chest.

2. Distinguish thoughts from experience. Thoughts
   might be, "I can't find my heartbeat," or "My
   heart is beating too fast," or "I worry I have a
   heart condition." Rather than judgment or analysis of your heartbeat, experience your heartbeat,
   become aware of its rhythm. How does it feel
   thumping against the palm of your hand?

3. Like finding the beat in a song, your awareness
   is less thought-focused ("Did I get that lyric
   right?") and more experience-focused ("Thump,
   thump, thump.").

4. Sense your chest rising and falling in rhythm with the sensation of your heart's beating. See if you can notice how your heartbeat decreases as you observe it or increases as you become caught up in your thoughts.

Keeping a record of your thoughts is a powerful strategy for breaking out of the anxiety spiral. Instead of those thoughts going around and around in your head, writing is a way to examine them in a more realistic, less emotional light. This kind of reflection puts you in control of your thoughts instead of your thoughts controlling you. Then you're no longer reacting to unrealistic, over-the-top thinking that only ramps up your anxiety.

Use this exercise when you become aware you're experiencing anxiety so you can get better at catching your thoughts early, before they mushroom. This strategy also helps when revisiting an anxious moment after the fact.

Identify a situation/interaction/image/thought stream that brings about anxiety for you.

- What is/was the hardest thing about this situation?

- What is/was your fear in this situation?

- What is/was your imagined worst-case scenario?

- What thoughts were running through your mind during the event or after or even now as you revisit it?

- Rate how much you believe each of these thoughts. (Use a 1 to 10 scale, with 1 being you don't believe it at all, and 10 being you believe it completely.)

Come back to this exercise in a day or two, or even a few hours, and revisit how much you believe these thoughts now.

When Your Thoughts Work Against You

When we're caught up in anxious thinking, our thoughts *feel* entirely real and accurate and so they keep us keyed up. In truth, the anxious mind isn't so good at differentiating the real from the unreal. In this virtual world, we feel as anxious and frightened as we would if our fear was based on something really happening. However, in reality, nothing terrible is going on and there may be little, if any, chance our feared scenarios will ever happen.

There are a number of biases we're all prone to that intensify anxiety. Familiarizing yourself with these "errors in thinking" will help you catch exaggerated or inaccurate thought patterns. Here are a few of the more common ones:

All-or-nothing thinking: Things are all good or all bad; you are perfect or a failure.

Overgeneralizing: If something negative happens in one situation it means it will happen in all future, similar situations.

Catastrophizing: You look to the future with sweeping negativity and forecast disaster instead of more realistic possibilities.

Labeling: Applying a fixed, global label on yourself or others without including any context. ("I'm a loser," "I'm bad," "I'm inadequate," "I'm a burden.")

"Should"-ing and "must"-ing: You have rigid expectations for how you *should* or *must* act, and when these unreasonable expectations aren't met, you forecast horrendous consequences.

Each time you successfully identify an error in thinking, your anxiety will decrease because you're able to see the situation at hand more realistically, or at least entertain other possibilities.

STRATEGY: DOWNWARD ARROW TECHNIQUE

The downward arrow technique is effective for identifying what deeper belief you hold about yourself that is triggering—and driving—your anxious thoughts. In cognitive behavioral therapy, core beliefs are described as your most central thoughts about yourself and the meaning you ascribe to the normal difficulties we all face. When a core belief is activated, your brain switches into a mode in which you take in only information that supports the belief, and disregard anything that may challenge it. This traps you in a feedback loop of biased thoughts generated by that core belief.

When you're caught up in negative core beliefs, it becomes difficult to think realistically about the events in your life. Learning to identify and challenge our core beliefs means these flawed ideas no longer make decisions for us.

Negative core beliefs typically fall into two general categories: beliefs associated with *helplessness* and beliefs associated with *unlovability*. See if any of the examples below sound familiar to you.

Examples of Helpless Core Beliefs

I'm a failure.

⇩

Nothing I do will make a difference.

⇩

I'm helpless.

⇩

I'm inadequate.

⇩

I'm weak.

Examples of Unlovable Core Beliefs

I'm unworthy.

⇩

I'm bad.

⇩

I'm unlikable.

⇩

I'm unwanted.

⇩

I'm not good enough.

The downward arrow technique helps you look beneath the surface of your anxious thoughts to see what's really driving them. To find your core beliefs, record your anxious thoughts, and then ask yourself, "If that thought were true, what would it mean about me as a person?"

Let's use Ava's anxious thoughts as an example:

"I'm worried I'm not going to complete my report for work on time. I second-guess my every move. I literally can't stop obsessing about work even for a few moments."

Here is the downward arrow technique:

What does it mean about you as a person if you don't complete the report?

"That I'm letting my team down."

⇩

What does it mean about you if you let your team down?

"My colleagues won't respect me."

⇩

What does it mean about you if your colleagues don't respect you?

⇩

"That I failed."

This reflects a helplessness core belief. Deep down, Ava believes she is inadequate as a person. Likely she is underestimating her competence (more on this later).

Get your notebook and try the following exercise to get at your core beliefs.

Identify a situation/interaction/image/thought stream that brings about anxiety for you.

1. Record the fearful/anxious thoughts you have about, or when you're in, the situation/interaction/image/thought stream (or revisit what you logged for the "Record Your Thoughts" strategy on page 154).

2. For each thought listed, ask yourself, "If this thought were true, what does it mean about me as a person?"

3. Each time you understand what that thought means about you, write it down.

4. Then ask yourself the same question about new thoughts listed: "What does it mean about me as a person if this thought is actually 100 percent accurate?" Then do the same for the next new thought. Eventually you will funnel down to a core belief.

Let's look at another example of the technique in action, this time with Ahmed. When talking with others, Ahmed appears calm and collected, but internally he is evaluating his every word. While on a date or social outing, he believes he appears awkward. The downward arrow technique follows:

What does it mean about you as a person if your date thinks you're awkward?

"I messed up. I lost that opportunity."

⇩

What does it mean about you if you messed up an opportunity with that date?

"That people will keep giving up on me."

⇩

What does it mean about you if people keep giving up on you?

"That I disappoint people."

⇩

What does it mean about you if you disappoint people?

⇩

"That no one is going to want me."

This reflects an unlovability core belief. Deep down, Ahmed believes no one is going to love him.

After you use the downward arrow technique with a number of your anxious thoughts, you will see certain core beliefs showing up repeatedly. The next step is to start challenging these deeply rooted ideas you carry about yourself.

STRATEGY: TEST YOUR CORE BELIEFS

In this exercise I'm going to push you out of your comfort zone so you can see if your core beliefs are as accurate as they feel to you. I want you to literally go out in the world and test your core beliefs—see if they actually hold up to reality.

If you realize that at the root of your anxious thinking is a deep fear that you're unlovable, go out and talk to others, join a group, make a point to spend time regularly with someone, or even ask close others if they like you.

If you recognize a core belief that you're incompetent/helpless, go out and take on a new but doable task: Sign up for a class,

create something, clean your house, organize a closet, build or fix
something, read a book to completion.

As you enter the situation, insert a different thought
(even if you don't quite believe it yet!). It could be as
simple as "I'm capable," or "I can be liked."

Be open to new information and to what you might
be overlooking that went well or differently from
how you expected. Then modify your beliefs about
yourself accordingly.

Go Deeper

Identifying Negative Thought Patterns

Developing awareness of your negative thought patterns will help you take the steps needed to make you feel better sooner. When you become aware that you're experiencing anxiety, stop and take stock. Write your answers in your notebook so you can delve into them.

- What is a scenario that is anxiety-inducing for me, including situations, interactions, events, and images?

    Example: Every time my boss is short with me, I withdraw because I feel anxious and worried that I'm not in good standing at work.

- What anxious thoughts am I having (or did I have) about this scenario?

    He doesn't like me.

    He's going to give me less work and make me unessential.

    I'm going to be rendered useless at work.

- How might my thoughts be distorted (label "errors in thinking")?

    Catastrophizing

    Overgeneralizing

    All-or-nothing thinking

- What does it mean about me as a person if my most fearful thoughts are true?

    I'll lose my job.

    I'll be embarrassed.

    I won't meet work goals.

    People will know I'm incompetent.

- What core belief was triggered?

    Helplessness

- How can I test out my core belief to see if I'm missing some information?

    The next time my boss is short with me, I won't withdraw but instead will ask questions about what he's looking for to see if I've missed anything.

Worry impacts our emotions in a big way. It influences what we do and how we feel physically. We can come to exist in an exhausted, tense-muscled state. This hyperarousal leads to irritability, difficulty sleeping, and eventually, even depression.

Here's a common example I see often in my psychology practice: A client, Emma, had a repetitive worry that she was in danger of being kicked out of her graduate program. Each time something went wrong with an assignment or she received an average grade, a chain of uncontrollable thoughts would ensue. She was afraid her professors thought she was incompetent. She second-guessed herself in class and when she spoke out was extremely self-conscious. Then she worried about what the other students thought of her. Emma believed she wasn't as intellectually competent as her peers. She would beat herself up for always worrying: "What's wrong with me? I'm so crazy. I can't stop worrying!"

No matter how hard Emma worked to push them away, the worried thoughts kept swirling up, again and again. Even peaceful rest was impossible. She would wake in the middle of the night harried by her concerns and then be unable to fall back to sleep. Exhausted from school and worrying, she didn't take care of herself, eat right, or exercise regularly. As a result, she also fretted about her physical health and began to think she had a serious medical illness.

We all worry on some level, but it becomes disproportionate when it's persistent and uncontrollable. When this happens, we lose time to an internal, not real-to-life focus. This hyperinternal focus is a vortex where no new energy or perspectives are allowed in. The vortex distorts reality and creates greater fear.

Excessive worrying is not problem-solving and is not productive. In fact, the exhaustion and emotional depletion actually makes us less productive. We aren't able to concentrate, plan accordingly, and make the best use of our energy and resources. And once again, we're robbed of the present moment.

We typically come to recognize we're in a vortex when the anxiety is intense. At this point, it can be quite difficult to escape. The quickest solution is to avoid this stage altogether. Developing an early warning awareness that reacts before anxiety has reached high intensity protects us from becoming stuck in the vortex.

STRATEGY: IDENTIFY YOUR WORRY TRIGGERS

Even though we tend to worry about the same things day in and day out, we persist in wasting time and energy considering each worry that pops up as if it were new and deeply significant. Our worries repeat because we fail to problem solve and cope with them appropriately. Identifying the larger issues your worried thoughts trigger means you can switch from worried thinking to problem-solving.

Below is a list of the more common larger issues that individual worries tend to trigger, and example steps/actions to take to address each. Identify the categories your worries tend to fall into and see if you can come up with a few steps to take for each.

Financial

> **Actionable step:** Develop a budget; meet with financial planner

Job/school

> **Actionable step:** Enroll in a class; get tutor

Achieving goals

> **Actionable step:** Review expectations; are they too high, too low?

Parenting

> **Actionable step:** Read parenting book; take parenting class

Health of self

> **Actionable step:** Get yearly medical physical with blood work

Health of others

> **Actionable step:** Work to accept uncertainty; I can only control so much

Relationships

> **Actionable step:** Read relationship self-help book

Diet/exercise

Actionable step: Meet with nutritionist; start walking twice a week

Self-image

Actionable step: Build self-esteem through volunteering; go to weekly psychotherapy

General safety of the world/community (politics, terrorism, environment)

Actionable step: Volunteer for political candidate who espouses my beliefs

If mentally replaying worries made you feel better, you wouldn't keep hashing out the same old sets of worries. Shift your attention from specific worried thoughts to considering how you could take an actionable step toward improving the larger issue(s).

STRATEGY: PROBABLE VS. POSSIBLE OUTCOMES

When we are caught in anxiety quicksand, each and every worrisome thought may seem acute and reasonable. Stress hormones are released, anxiety builds, and it becomes difficult to distinguish the *probable* from the *possible*. Instead of repeating the same concerns over and over in your head, write out the following for each of your uneasy thoughts:

- What is the worst possible scenario that I'm afraid of happening regarding this thought?

- What is the best possible scenario that I wish could happen regarding this thought?

- What is a realistic scenario that will likely happen regarding this thought?

You can be at peace. Slow down and train your mind to steer away from far-reaching catastrophe and toward thoughts that represent the realistic, and most likely, outcomes.

STRATEGY: PRODUCTIVE VS. UNPRODUCTIVE WORRY

Another helpful strategy when worry thoughts become triggered is to consider how productive (useful, helpful in your life or to you) it is to worry about that particular issue. When you recognize you're worrying, classify worried thoughts as productive or unproductive based on the following checklist.

Productive

- ☐ My worry is in regard to a specific problem.
- ☐ My worry is about something I'm going to have to deal with in the near or immediate future.
- ☐ I have some control over the situation's outcome.
- ☐ I can make a choice or decision that will solve the worry.

☐ This is a new worry, something I don't usually think about.

☐ There's an actionable step I can take to help alleviate my worry.

Unproductive

☐ I'm worried about something uncertain in the future that no one knows whether it will occur.

☐ I have no control over this worry.

☐ I think about possible ways to deal with the worry, but nothing feels good enough.

☐ I'm obsessively focused and can't stop thinking about this worry.

☐ This is a recurrent worry of mine.

☐ There is no action I can take to solve this worry.

If your worry seems to fall more into the "unproductive" category, the next time it pops up, remind yourself that it's okay to live with some uncertainties. In fact, it's impossible *not* to. Remember to practice acceptance of things as they are. On the other hand, if your worry is productive, make a plan for how you want to problem solve the situation at hand. (There's more on problem-solving in chapter 9.)

Overgeneralizing and Underestimating

When we experience normal anxiety, we focus on the immediate concerns and challenges that no one is immune to, e.g., "Thanksgiving with the family is going to be hard to get through this year." The highly anxious mind compounds these difficulties by extending them out across time and over a variety of situations: "Every time I'm with my family, I get stressed out." Even worse, the anxious mind convinces us that we won't be able to cope with the thing we dread: "I can't go to any more family functions, it's too upsetting." As a result, we spin our wheels trying to prevent feared situations, emotions, and/or interactions by avoiding people and events that don't actually pose a real threat. Of course, in reality, there's only so much control we have over the course of events, and so all this anxious energy results in us feeling at the mercy of life, powerless, and desperate to find relief.

When we overgeneralize, we develop conclusions about ourselves, our emotions, and what we can and can't do based on a single experience. For instance, Carmen found out she didn't get her desired work promotion and concludes: "I'll never get promoted." Nolan had a couple of unfulfilling dates and concludes: "I'll never meet the right one."

Overgeneralizing causes you to seal the deal on your fate. In your mind, you render your future chances of success or getting what you want at zero. And perhaps most importantly, overgeneralizing means an end to trying. For example, if you stop believing you will ever get promoted, you stop putting in the extra effort at work.

If you believe you won't find a romantic partner, you stop trying to engage new acquaintances or actively date.

The second component of the anxious mind is that we underestimate our ability to cope if what we fear actually happens. We tell ourselves we can't possibly manage the frightening situation our mind is generating: "No way, I wouldn't even know what to do," "I won't be able to deal with that," "That would kill me," "I'd go crazy." In the face of a possible adversity, we imagine ourselves melting into a puddle of anxious fear. This reinforces the superstitious notion that worry itself will keep us safe: "If I worry enough, I'll be okay," "If I obsess over this project, I'll work harder," "If I keep myself upset and on edge about this, I'll be better prepared when it happens."

This pattern can be broken. You're capable of managing far more than you imagine. Just because you don't want to deal with something, or it may be hard to deal with, doesn't mean you can't be effective. You have already managed quite a bit in your life. You just do it; you push through to the other side.

Go
Deeper

Challenging Overgeneralization

Perhaps you're recognizing some of your anxious thinking represents overgeneralization. Nonetheless, you still can't get the fear or thought out of your mind. Start challenging those overgeneralizations. When you hit a setback, ask yourself the following questions—and write your responses down, if you can.

1. Can you think of a time in the past when your conclusion has not been true?

2. Can you imagine a time or instance in the future when your conclusion may not be true?

3. How probable, from 0 to 100 percent, do you feel it is that the fear you're thinking about is going to actually happen?

4. What do you gain by believing this thought? For example, do you believe it keeps you safe in some way?

5. What consequences may come from believing this thought? For example, will you give up trying to get what you desire, allowing a self-fulfilling prophecy to result?

STRATEGY: SPOT OVERGENERALIZING

As we've seen, our worries and catastrophic thoughts often repeat. We sometimes have new ones, but generally similar ones repeat over time and reflect the core beliefs we hold about ourselves. Open your notebook back to the thoughts recorded earlier in this chapter.

Underline or put a checkmark by the thoughts that reflect a tendency to overgeneralize. Clues that you might be overgeneralizing include:

- Taking one example of something upsetting and believing that example will occur again and again in a variety of contexts.

- Extreme language: "This *always* happens," "It will *never* be okay," "No one will *ever* like me," "I'll *never* win," "I am *always* the slowest," "I'm the dumb one."

- When you hit a setback or receive negative feedback, you have thoughts about giving up and putting less effort in to reach your goals.

Try this visualization exercise:

1. Think through one of your more upsetting thoughts or worst-case scenarios. In your mind's eye, play out the details of what you fear as if it is really happening. Imagine where you are, whom you are interacting with, or what news you're getting.

2. Now imagine your worst-case blocks, setbacks, or embarrassments, but visualize yourself effectively coping with what you're feeling or the other feared obstacles.

3. Instead of freaking out, giving up, or becoming painfully uncomfortable with anxiety or fear, you stick with the situation. You challenge yourself to find a way to effectively deal with your biggest fear.

4. Imagine you use a strategy (take a few deep breaths, use internal supportive language, remind yourself of your larger goals) and it works. You show yourself that you can cope. You find a way through the circumstances and emerge in a more comfortable and thoughtful place.

Practice this exercise and you will be much better equipped to deal with the real thing.

WRAP-UP

- Become an observer of, not a reactor to, your thoughts.

- Keep a thought record to develop awareness of your anxious-thought patterns.

- Make anxious thoughts less threatening by identifying errors in thinking, core beliefs, worry triggers, and overgeneralizations.

- Increase your awareness for problem-solving versus unproductive worry.

- When anxious about a future possibility, ask yourself, "Am I underestimating my competence and/or overgeneralizing?"

CHAPTER NINE

Getting Unstuck from Thoughts

Changing Your Self-Talk

Anxiety increases in intensity when a person's internal narrative is filled with harsh judgments around good and bad, right and wrong. What we say to ourselves influences how we think about ourselves, what we communicate to others, and how much we believe in our competence and worth. Anxiety is further amplified when a person's internal narrative is overloaded with generalizations—always, never, forever, everything, nothing. Consider which of the following two statements is laden with greater intensity:

1. "I suck, I'll never get a life."

2. "I'm lonely and need to work on building social skills."

The latter is hopeful. It acknowledges the emotion but also identifies a specific skill that could be developed to help with the feeling of loneliness.

If you're struggling with anxiety, there's a strong chance your internal commentary is overly critical and harsh. But perhaps your anxious thoughts and behaviors about situations and events have more to do with the critical reaction you anticipate from others, and less to do with the situations themselves.

Imagine a friend who, every time you hit a setback, tells you what you did to cause the problem and reminds you of all the times in the past you did the same "bad" thing. That is likely how you're treating yourself. People who make us feel good about ourselves and comfortable being ourselves are the ones we are most at ease with. Start relating to yourself in the way a warm, kind friend or family member would. Changing the voice in your head to be more self-supportive and nurturing will give you a bit of comfort—or padding, if you will—when negative, anxious thoughts kick in.

STRATEGY: BECOME AWARE OF YOUR SELF-TALK

How we speak to ourselves has a significant impact on anxiety. Yet we let our anxious self-talk play out again and again on autopilot. Think about the following questions regarding your self-talk so you can make the voice in your head more nurturing and less judgmental.

- What is the tone of your internal dialogue? Is it loud and impatient, or is it warm and tolerant of what's going on with you and your immediate world?

- When you're upset, does your internal voice try to soothe you? Or does it use intense/judgmental language that makes you feel worse, such as, "That was bad," "You suck," "You're never going to get this right," "People hate you," "You're a loser."

- Does your internal voice take away your moments of joy? When you're happy or feel at ease, does your voice intrude, telling you things you need to work on, tasks that need to be accomplished, or fearful possibilities?

- Are there certain tasks, hobbies, or people that bring out a kinder, warmer side of you, where your internal voice seems softer, less critical? If so, these are the things you should do more of and the types of relationships you should cultivate. If not, experiment with different activities and people to find those that bring out your softer side.

Cultivate your capacity for ease and calm, and encourage self-talk that is compassionate and forgiving. Self-compassion means showing yourself a warm understanding of your perceived inadequacies, including your struggle with anxiety. Forgiveness means voicing a kinder internal monologue when you encounter a setback or notice your shortcomings.

STRATEGY: PINK UNICORNS

Write a few sentences about developing compassionate self-talk while not thinking about pink unicorns. Whatever you do, stick to the task of writing about developing a compassionate internal narrative, but make sure NOT to think about pink unicorns. Pink unicorns should be nowhere in your mind when you do this task. Each time you think about a pink unicorn, mark an X in your notebook.

How did it go? Were you able to not think of pink unicorns? Probably you were not and here's why: Telling ourselves to not think about something has entirely the opposite effect. This is partly why it's so frustrating when we're upset and a well-meaning friend or loved one says, "Stop thinking about that," or "Everything is fine, stop worrying."

Daniel Wegner, a renowned social psychologist in thought suppression at Harvard University, asked lab participants to verbally share their thoughts while being sure to not call to mind the thought of a white bear. The participants were asked to ring a bell each time they thought of a white bear. Even though they were instructed to push away the thought, on average, they brought to mind the thought of a white bear more than once per minute.

When we suppress thoughts, we essentially tell ourselves to "stop thinking about that!" The mind then monitors itself for each time it does think about "that" and then brings "that" to our conscious awareness. Instead of criticizing yourself to stop thinking or worrying about this or that, consider challenging the thoughts that bring on anxiety.

STRATEGY: REPLACE NEGATIVE THOUGHTS

When you have a thought that keeps repeating in your internal narrative, pull out this thought record.

1. What triggered the thought? What were you doing or imagining when the thought occurred to you?
   Example: Considering an invitation to a neighborhood potluck.

2. What is the thought(s) that accompanies this trigger?
   Example: "No one will talk to me." "I'll feel like an outsider." "I'll feel insecure."

3. Label the emotion(s) you feel when you have these thoughts and the intensity of each

emotion on a scale of 1 (less intensity) to 10 (extreme intensity).

Example: "Inadequate: 5, weak: 6, anxious: 9, dread: 9."

4. Is there anything that is not supportive of the thought(s) in #2?

Example: "They invited me to the party, so someone wants me there." "I do make small talk with the neighbors from time to time." "I live in the same neighborhood, so we at least have that in common."

5. Can you think of a replacement thought that might be less negative but still realistic?

Example: "Even if people aren't including me in every conversation, I was invited, and I live in the same neighborhood so I'm not a total outsider."

6. Revisit the feelings listed in #3. Rate each one when keeping this new thought in mind. Recognize if the feeling(s) decreased in intensity, even if only by a notch or two.

Example: "Inadequate: 2, weak: 5, anxious: 7, dread: 7."

Each time the negative thought enters your conscious awareness, compassionately acknowledge it: "I see you, negative thinking." Then bring to mind a more *realistic* thought: "Well, at least they invited me."

Problem-Solving

In psychology, the tendency to work through negative events by replaying them again and again in one's mind is called *rumination*. Rumination refers to internally focusing on anxiety/upset, as well as all the reasons, causes, future possibilities, or risks that could occur due to this distress. An example might be sitting alone, thinking about feeling behind your peers academically and employment wise. Then your mind turns to worrying the situation will never improve and imagining a future of always feeling inadequate and professionally lacking. Next, you self-criticize about why this happened in the first place. And then you may begin to look for ways to avoid people who might ask questions about what you do for a living or where you went to college.

Many people worry because they believe they are problem-solving and engaging in a constructive process about the issues they face. Reminding yourself of what is or could be of concern comes to be seen as a way of avoiding denial and catastrophe.

In fact, rumination is essentially a passive process that leads only to more anxious thinking. Overthinking, alone in your mind, leaves no room for other perspectives or effective problem-solving.

Brainstorming

Take a more active, direct approach to working through your worries. Brainstorming is a technique whereby you take the pressure off yourself by acknowledging that there is no "correct" decision to make or a "right" way to solve your issue.

1. Pick an issue that you worry about on a regular basis or a new worry that has come to mind. Write down a few sentences about the area of concern.

2. Now write down as many ideas as you can think of for how you could manage the issue. Pay no mind to how outlandish or impractical the ideas might be. There are no rules other than to let the creative juices flow.

3. The goal here is to open up your process and escape repetitive thought patterns. In fact, try to think of ridiculous solutions. This can actually reduce the seriousness you may feel about the particular worry. One client I worked with was struggling with how to deal with a difficult roommate and came up with

the thought, "Every time she annoys me I'm going to make a joke." At first this seemed silly to her, but the idea worked because it decreased her tension and helped her not take the roommate so seriously.

4. Once you have a number of various solutions, think how each possible solution would help or hinder the problem. Some things will feel impossible and others will feel as if they barely help. Pick one that is reasonably doable.

5. Then take an actionable step; actively do something to relieve your anxiety over this particular issue.

Whenever you find yourself anxious or worried, notice
if you're feeling that life and others are against you.
Even if your blame is warranted, wallowing in it is not
going to help you achieve your goals or make you feel
any better. What will help you feel better is focusing on
what is within your control. Letting go of feeling at the
mercy of life or circumstance creates a feeling of safety
and calmness. Here is a way to no longer face hardship
with helplessness:

1. Pick an anxious thought or worry trigger.

2. Recognize the thoughts that keep you in a helpless state over this particular worry:
   "I'll never find a way," "It will always be like this."

3. Come up with three actionable steps you can take
   and that are within your control.

4. Take action.

For example, Layla was anxious about an upcoming
wedding she had to attend. She had lost touch with
many of the folks invited to the wedding and felt overwhelmed by worries over what they would think of her
and how she would be socially on the outside. In order
to move away from wallow and worry toward healthy
control, she asked herself what she could do to improve
the situation.

- Reach out to old friends before the wedding. Text, call, write a note.

Layla connected a bit before the event and even video chatted with one friend.

- Imagine the day going the way you would like it to.

Layla visualized herself the day of the wedding being present and in the moment. She imagined awkward encounters, or even feeling on the outside, but in her visualization, she was able to cope and manage the situation effectively. She visualized feeling proud of herself at the end of the event.

- Practice deep breathing, yoga, or mindfulness meditation.

Layla practiced mindful breathing for 10 minutes a day leading up to the event.

> IMPORTANT NOTE: *An actionable item can be accepting a situation as it is and doing nothing. Then each time the fear comes to mind, practice acceptance instead of rumination.*

Sometimes, clearly seeing the consequences for you of a worried mind-set can motivate you to let go of the worry and come back to the present moment. With this goal in mind, conduct a cost-benefit analysis of how beneficial it is to you to continue to experience anxiety over whatever it is you're ruminating or obsessing on. Write out the consequences and benefits of worrying about a specific issue.

Example:

Costs to keeping anxiety a focus

I'm removed from the present.

⇩

I feel bad.

⇩

I'm keyed up and physically ill at ease.

⇩

I'm stuck.

I won't be surprised if the bad thing I worry about happens.

⇩

I will be vigilant, which protects me.

Decide which cost you're most willing to accept and which option brings you closer to your long-term goal of having more peace and less anxiety in your life.

NOTE: *It can be quite effective to examine the costs and benefits after anxiety has lessened. Once the intensity decreases, your brain has the bandwidth to problem solve and take on a broader perspective.*

You Are Not Your Thoughts

While visiting an amusement park with my young son, I became highly anxious over his enthusiastic desire for me to accompany him on an old, rickety roller coaster. As he happily pulled me into the line, worried thoughts gripped me: "It's rickety and old, what if it jumps the track?" "What if the harness breaks when it goes upside down?" "What if the safety mechanisms fail?" "What if they haven't kept up with standards and regulations?" "What if . . . What if . . . What if . . . " Within a matter of minutes, I fully believed catastrophe would strike if we rode the roller coaster. I wanted to stop us both from taking the plunge.

Suddenly, as if waking from a trance, I saw the ride operator open the door to our roller coaster car and we hopped aboard. As the machine accelerated, the fearful thoughts began to retreat into the background of my awareness. There was an opening now for more than worry.

I became aware of my son's liveliness and pure elation. Seeing him throw his hands up in the air, laughing and smiling. I felt it, too; it was exhilarating to go against my fearful thoughts. The thoughts were not gone, but I was no longer a captive of them. I was energized. I was present. I was in the moment. I was a person who, along with worried thoughts, was having a thrilling, memorable experience.

Similar to watching an engrossing movie, a particular thought stream has the potential to pull us in so entirely that there is no "us" separate from those thoughts. The thoughts become all-powerful, making choices for us, limiting our experiences, telling us what's right and what's wrong. It's only through breaking the trance that we can come to see the nature of things as they truly are.

Our brains supply us with an inordinate number of thoughts, many of which are unhelpful and even downright inaccurate. Taking each one seriously would be like visiting a beautiful beach and spending the entire time counting the grains of sand.

Perhaps up until this point, you've not even considered your thoughts as anything other than a literal reflection of your reality. When a thought enters, you take it seriously. You feel it, you worry about it, and perhaps even begin to plan based on it. Accepting thoughts at face value leads to fusing your identity with whatever you're thinking in a particular moment.

There should be a space between you, the observer you, and the thoughts your mind drops on you. You're not your thoughts. You're the leader, the conductor, the captain— the one who oversees and observes—your thought stream.

STRATEGY: BECOME AN OBSERVER

Observing your thoughts and feelings is similar to standing on a high rock to watch the sea and reflect on its many changes. You notice the ocean waves, turbulent at times, peaceful at others, and often somewhere in the middle. From the safety of your rock it's easy to label what you're observing. You do not experience yourself as the changes. You are the one noticing the changes.

Even in a hurricane, the sea eventually becomes calm again. Observe yourself. Recognize that even though your brain might be spinning with various anxiety-based scenarios, it will eventually return to a more peaceful pattern. And a peaceful brain will inevitably become unsettled again. The feelings or thoughts that dominate the mind moment by moment eventually evaporate to be replaced by new feelings and thoughts. Such is the nature of the mind.

1. Sit quietly. Imagine the observing part of yourself as separate from your thoughts and emotions.

2. Notice the direction your mind roams and the accompanying physical sensations in your body.

3. Perhaps you notice tension in your chest, sweaty palms, or you have a headache.

4. Label these specific sensations without merging your identity or sense of self with them. For example, "I notice tension and worry coming over me" as opposed to "I'm a nervous wreck."

If you keep practicing, you'll find that thoughts, emotions, and sensations pass, only to be replaced by others. Calm invariably returns. Your thoughts will not frighten you when you recognize that they are temporary and not a direct reflection of reality.

Go Deeper

The Anxiety Struggle

Cultivate your capacity for ease and calm by seeing the bigger picture of how much your struggle with anxiety has come to limit and define you.

Write a paragraph about your anxious identity. How does your struggle with anxiety influence who you are as a person? How did your anxiety struggle start and what perpetuated your anxiety over time? How do you feel your anxiety will hold you back in life? What kind of person do you see yourself as, as a result of your anxiety struggle?

You can let this struggle go. Consider how your identity would shift if you were able to better cope with your anxiety.

Write a second paragraph, again with the realities of what you have endured but this time within the context that you have given up the struggle with anxiety. You accept your anxiety; it is what it is. At the same time, imagine you have found ways to manage and effectively cope. You are able to experience joy, be present, and connect with others. What kind of person would you see yourself as if anxiety no longer dominated your life?

Our sense of our ability to grow changes depending on how we perceive our circumstances. Start seeing yourself as someone who can (like countless others!) recover from anxiety.

This strategy helps you observe and be aware of your experience without becoming overwhelmed by it.

1. Imagine yourself safely on an elevated platform in the middle of a large train station. You have a bird's-eye view of each track and see each train as it enters and leaves your station. You see some trains reenter the station after just a few minutes. Other trains take longer to reenter, while others don't come back at all. Some trains stick around for a bit before they head back out of the station. Other trains leave immediately after arriving.

2. Imagine your thoughts as these trains. You are the one safely observing the thoughts come and go. Some thoughts linger, others leave quickly. You have no control or urgency or job responsibility around this other than to be aware of your thoughts as you would the trains entering and exiting the station.

3. Similar to "red train" or "green train," see if you can label each train (thought) as it comes in and out of the station (your mind). Without judgment or criticism, list in your notebook, or say aloud, the thoughts that come through your station. See if you can group the thoughts into larger categories: "worried thoughts," "catastrophic thoughts,"

"family thoughts," "self-esteem thoughts,"
"future thoughts," or "work thoughts." Each time
you label a thought as belonging to a certain category, that thought becomes less persuasive and
less significant.

Test Your Predictions

Do you ever wonder why we tend to put our attention
more into negative thoughts than positive ones? Or why
we can still remember a critical comment or upsetting
interaction weeks or even years after the event? The
"negativity bias" is the term used to describe the fact
that undesirable thoughts, emotions, and interactions
have a greater impact on how we feel than do positive
or neutral events. In fact, research shows that people are
much better at remembering negative versus positive
things, including angry versus happy faces, and take
more time and mental energy processing negative events
than positive ones. This bias is part of our evolutionary
wiring. From a survival standpoint, the cost of overlooking a negative is far greater than the cost of overlooking
a positive. Consider the early man who overlooks a bush
loaded with edible berries. He will probably survive the
mistake, but if he fails to look over his shoulder to see a
stalking wolf pack, he may not.

You can see how negativity bias helped our ances-
tors survive. But in today's world, when few of us face
real threats in our daily lives, this bias can result in

lots of needless—and exhausting—worry. When we become overly anxious, the negativity bias is often the behind-the-scenes culprit. We scan our environment and ourselves for possible threats and then, without thoughtful reflection, make improbable forecasts of bad outcomes.

You can break away from the habitually unhelpful ways you see yourself and your world by turning each negative thought into a prediction to be tried out and tested.

STRATEGY: WHAT'S YOUR ANXIETY TELLING YOU?

When you experience anxious thinking, it likely stops you in your tracks because you take it as a signal or even a command for you to worry and ruminate. This may be your negativity bias operating at full tilt.

What if the anxious thinking is not a signal to stop and wring your hands but rather a sign that something you really care about or desire is at stake? When you recognize you're making anxious predictions, complete the following statements to see what might be on the other side of the anxiety for you and then test out your prediction.

1. Write down an anxious prediction (or thought).

   Example: "If I drive, I'll have a panic attack. Yet I haven't seen my mother in a long time. I worry all the time about why I can't drive. I also beat myself up for being so weak."

2. Write down why this matters to you.

   Example: "I want to visit my elderly mother and spend time with her. She lives in a nursing home over an hour away, so I have to drive. I've already missed out on so much time with her, but I can't deal with the panic."

3. Write down strategies that might help you.

   Example: Practice progressive muscle relaxation, deep breathing, guided imagery (imagine driving and being able to cope and arrive safely). Practice positive self-talk ("I can and I will drive and see her").

4. Test out the anxious prediction; see if your hypothesis was accurate.

   Example: "I drove to my mom's nursing home and I was uncomfortable but did not lose control and did not have a panic attack and I got to see my mom!"

Here are specific ways to test common anxious predictions so you can start working on yours.

WHAT ANXIETY TELLS YOU	HOW TO TEST IT
I'm afraid the airplane will crash and I will die.	Practice relaxation exercises, visualization, deep breathing and then take a flight.
I'm worried about people not liking me, and being rejected.	Go to a party, work event, neighborhood function, and try to interact with people. Ask questions; don't let yourself recede into a corner.
I'll never be successful.	Take on a new class, work project, hobby. Build something, take care of a plant, start a garden.
I'll never be loved.	Ask family if they love you (it still counts even if it's family!). Or become a pet owner; pets provide unconditional love to many.
The world is against me.	Notice the little things: light traffic, good weather, a kind person helping you in some way. Catch the world when it's being good to you.
I'm useless.	Do something that makes you feel competent: build a garden, take care of an elderly person or a child, offer to help someone in your neighborhood, clean your place of residence, clean your car, plan an activity of some sort and follow through.

Now take one of your anxious predictions, remind yourself of why it matters to you that you work through it, pick a strategy that will help you, and go out in the world and test it out!

WRAP-UP

- Train the voice in your head toward self-compassion and self-acceptance.

- Replace anxious and negative thoughts with realistic thoughts.

- Make goals and take actionable steps to lessen anxious rumination.

- Go out in the world, test out your anxious predictions, and see if they're accurate.

CHAPTER TEN

Putting the Tools to Work

Whether you've struggled with anxiety all of your life, or if this is your first time, you've likely had hopeless moments along the way. Your anxious thinking may make you doubt your ability to progress. It's no wonder you feel this way, because anxiety can become like a part of your identity, or a shadow you simply can't shake. Here are ways to take the strategies you're reading about and form longer-term habits that will lead you away from hopeless thinking and toward the satisfying life you want and deserve.

From Strategies to Habits

If you continue to cultivate your skills for finding ease and calm when anxiety is triggered, eventually your anxiety patterns will begin to break, and in the spaces that open up you can cultivate new habits of thinking and responding. It's important to remember that changing the brain's wiring takes time and consistent practice. It's just when we think we can't take it anymore and want to give up that we make our biggest gains. Eventually, for longer and longer periods of time, you'll forget that you're practicing healthy coping. Instead, you'll enjoy the breeze on your face and the experience of living in this life now.

Consider what can come if you continue to do this work. Perhaps your baseline anxiety level, what you feel most of the time, was at a 6 on a 1 to 10 scale (1 is entirely relaxed and 10 is full anxiety meltdown). Once these strategies become habits you'll find that your baseline drops, so now perhaps it is more like a 3 or a 4. This is a marked difference and is the payoff for all your effort. Once your overall anxiety level decreases, even if only by a few notches, it will become even easier and faster to successfully challenge distressing thoughts and repetitive thinking.

Take a moment as you conclude this section to tune into your internal voice. Is it chastising you that you should do more or reminding you of what you are doing wrong or criticizing your lack of commitment? Remember, you do not have to do anything written in this book. There is not a "right" or "wrong" or "should" or "shouldn't" approach to take you out of your anxiety struggle. What *will* take you out of it is making a choice for yourself. Do you want to live in a different way? You would not be engaging these strategies on any level if the answer wasn't yes. So make a commitment to yourself to work on your anxiety each day, no matter how small the effort. When you miss a day, just pick right back up, no judgment, no criticizing, just pure, clear, persistent determination.

Planning

Review the planning you started in chapter 4 (page 67) and revised in chapter 7 (page 135). Reconsider how well your planning system is working. Have you followed through with the plans you made for yourself regarding implementing the strategies?

Consider adding to your planning approach a couple of reminders each day on your phone or digital calendar. You might have the reminder "breathe" in order to stay relaxed and mindful. Or the reminder "positive self-talk" to be aware of how you're speaking to yourself in your own head.

Review what you learned in the last two chapters. Identify which strategies you want to incorporate into your current plan. Try to do your anxiety work at the same time or times each day. A precise time provides a cue for the brain that will hasten the "neurons-that-fire-together-wire-together" process.

Track Your Progress

One of the most powerful ways to make a new behavior into a habit is to track what you're doing. It's essential to long-term progress that you set up a system where you track on a daily basis the strategies you're using, and the intensity of your anxiety. As we've seen previously, you can quickly and easily track progress with a

STRATEGY	MON	TUES
"Thinking about" vs. "Experiencing"	✓	
Record Your Thoughts		
Downward Arrow Technique		
Test Your Core Beliefs		
Identify Your Worry Triggers		
Probable vs. Possible Outcomes		
Unproductive vs. Productive Worry		
Spot Overgeneralizing		✓
Stop Underestimating Your Competence		
Become Aware of Your Self-Talk		
Pink Unicorns		
Replace Negative Thoughts		
Un-Learn Helplessness		
Cost-Benefit Analysis		
Become an Observer		
Train Station		
What's Your Anxiety Telling You?		
Rate Your Anxiety on a 1 to 10 Scale	3	7

chart you sketch out in your notebook. Take a look at the example.

Each day, check any and all strategies you use from chapters 8 and 9, or make a version of this table based on the strategies most useful/applicable to you. Also, be sure to rate your anxiety, using a 1 to 10 scale, with 1 being entirely relaxed and 10 being full anxiety meltdown.

	WEDS	THURS	FRI	SAT	SUN
				✓
			✓		
		✓			
	✓				
				✓	
	9	2	7	5	3

Goal Setting

Struggling with anxiety can feel like fighting the ocean's current. We spend so much time working to stay afloat that we don't have the energy left to focus on actually getting somewhere. Operating in survival mode has some negative consequences, especially when it comes to anxiety management. First and foremost, survival mode doesn't lead to long-term progress in terms of consistently escaping the torment of anxiety. Also, survival mode keeps us stuck in a mental state where we're neither fully present nor able to enjoy the things we cherish most.

Take a break from treading water. Imagine yourself safely on a boat, even if only for a few moments. From this vantage point, you can observe your anxiety spiral without becoming entirely engulfed by it. With this perspective in mind, consider your goals for anxiety management:

- What made you pick up this book?

- What do you want to achieve?

- How do you want to feel on the inside?

- How do you wish you could cope with anxious thoughts?

People often get to this point and then start to doubt themselves, or talk themselves out of their goals because they fear it will be too hard to accomplish, or they're not strong enough to meet challenging tasks, or they will fail in the end. Remember, people like you all over the world have struggled with anxiety and have gotten better. It's not that they never feel anxious again, but they find methods to cope in healthy ways and stay present in their lives. Anxiety is treatable, perhaps more so than any other mental health problem, and people get better by consistently applying new ways of thinking and coping.

Setting a goal and sticking to it is akin to spotting and then reaching a buoy while treading water in the ocean. Each buoy leads to another and another and before you know it, you see the shore on the horizon. Putting the effort in and reaching for goals will almost instantaneously help you believe in yourself, increase your self-esteem, and make your anxiety seem less daunting.

STRATEGY OF THE DAY

Pick a few strategies from this section that you can incorporate on a daily basis, or a different specific focus each day. One example would be to label a day "Positive Self-Talk Day," where you're mindful of your internal narrative, or "Identify Errors in Thinking Day," where you commit to focusing on what exaggerated or irrational thought patterns may be making you feel anxious. Another helpful strategy is to "Become an Observer" (page 193) of your thoughts each day. If only for five minutes, commit to watching your thoughts go by without becoming attached or actively pushing them away.

STRATEGY OF THE WEEK

Pick a few overarching or general strategies that you can work into your weekly routine at least three times this week. They don't need to take a prolonged period of time, just something reasonably achievable for you in the context of your life. For example, you could incorporate the idea of "Un-Learn Helplessness" (page 188), where you commit to taking one reasonable, actionable step to combat what is making you anxious. Or commit to a hypothesis test and use it to challenge at least one of your anxious beliefs.

Go Deeper

Create Your Weekly Strategies Calendar

Revisit your weekly strategies calendar you created in chapters 4 (page 73) and 7 (page 141). Take a moment to look over the current month. If you have not already done so, write in work, social, and family commitments and appointments.

Habit formation comes faster when we teach our brain new strategies and techniques on a daily basis. Also, anxiety is reduced when we have a solid plan and stick to it. Write in one strategy from chapters 8 and 9 that you're willing to employ every day of the month.

Assess what is coming up by digitally or manually marking red, yellow, and green zones on your calendar. Red zones are those that are more anxiety charged, green are those where you expect to be fairly at ease and feel less internal pressure, and yellow are neutral where you imagine you will feel neither very anxious nor very relaxed.

Take a step back and consider which red zones might trigger anxious thinking for you. On days or times where you anticipate anxious thinking or see a red zone, write down a strategy (or strategies) that you think will be particularly suited for that specific trigger. For example, if you're anticipating a few events that will cause you to ruminate or overthink, consider keeping a thought record that week. Also, if you're dreading an encounter, consider if you're underestimating your competence and filtering out your abilities and strengths that can help you through the difficult situation.

Check-In

For the kind of change that really lasts for the long term, it's important to check in with yourself and see how you're progressing. Otherwise, you may fall back into those same old anxious habits. Checking in is a way to stay focused on your goals and to notice which strategies are working or which you may want to add or change.

Check in with yourself to take stock of what's going well and also what you've lost sight of on your path to a peaceful life. And as you also take stock of your setbacks, recommit to persevering. Rewiring the brain takes practice and time.

How Did You Do?

Start by reflecting on how you're doing every couple of days. Then as you notice your symptoms improving, check in once a week and then eventually monthly.

- How successful were you with your daily goals?

- How about your weekly goals?

- Based on the 1 to 10 scale, are you noticing any symptom improvement?

Improvement may be subtle at first, but any reduction in the intensity of your anxiety, even going from an 8 to a 7, is an improvement. If you weren't as successful as you'd like, try things differently. Swap out the strategies you've been using for others, and be honest about what's blocking you from making more progress. Remind yourself that you want this, and you can and will have peace of mind and a meaningful life.

STICKING WITH IT

Any time we make a change or learn something new, we experience disappointments and obstacles. When you hit setbacks, take a moment to consider what negative thoughts or beliefs you have about your ability to get better and start new techniques.

For example, you might have the thought, "Doing these exercises will improve my anxiety," and simultaneously think, "These exercises are hard, so I probably won't get anywhere." Consider incorporating more realistic thoughts. For example, "Other people have done this and made themselves better, so maybe I could change," or "I don't have to implement the strategies all the time or be perfect at it to improve."

Each day you're one step closer to your goal of emotional freedom. Don't give up. You will come out on the other side of your anxiety. What's on the other side? Ease within your body and your mind. The kind of ease that will enable you to steadily push out of your comfort zone so you no longer miss out on all life has to offer. You can and will achieve, connect, and live a fully present life.

Reading about the strategies means you're no longer resigning yourself to an anxious life. This change alone, of giving yourself new ways of thinking and managing your anxiety, perhaps more than any other, will deliver the peace and calm you deserve. Now keep going. Don't give up; you've already come so far.

staying
on track

What You'll Learn in This Section

Recognize that you do have the ability to manage your anxiety and experience the kind of ease and calm you want. This confidence doesn't have to come all at once. However, it's something we're all capable of building, and this section addresses how to stick with the strategies for the long term. One element is learning to celebrate your successes. Recognition of progress, even when it comes in very small increments, fuels your ability to be persistent, and persistence is the path to new learning. We will also look at how to sidestep the negativity bias, nip anxiety in the bud, and clarify which strategies you want to maintain throughout your life. And we will explore ways to accelerate your progress on the anxiety-reduction path—including building your support network, psychotherapy, and medication.

CHAPTER ELEVEN

The Road Ahead

Long-Term Outlook

It is estimated that one in five adults in the United States meets the diagnostic criteria for an anxiety disorder. As prevalent as anxiety is, it is also highly responsive to treatment. But how can we tell who will get better and who won't? Well, I see it consistently in my practice, and research backs this up: When people adopt these three "beliefs" they typically are able to learn, sooner rather than later, to manage their anxiety symptoms.

1. **Believe you need to change:** Doing the same things you've always done keeps you stuck. Open yourself up to new ways of thinking and behaving and you'll start changing.

2. **Believe in the strategies:** Self-doubt and second-guessing the process is only a distraction from building the new habits that will take you away from anxiety and toward greater calm. The strategies in this book are all evidence based,

which means research has proven their effectiveness. The strategies work, they really do!

3. **Believe in your ability to grow:** As we've seen, people just like you all over the world experience anxious patterns yet find sustained peace of mind, so why couldn't this be you? Believe in yourself, and you will gain control over your anxiety.

Your Biggest Victories So Far

Take a moment to remember what emotions and habits were ruling you before you read this book. Now, like playing back a reel of sports highlights, look at your greatest victories so far. Perhaps you couldn't connect with your other emotions, except for anxiety, and now you're no longer afraid to look under the anxiety and understand what you're really feeling. Or perhaps you've found ways to relax your body and not feel as physically keyed up.

Maybe you've stopped avoiding something, or a few things, that have long caused you fear and apprehension. Maybe the concept of acceptance, that anxiety is a part of human experience, has opened up space so there's a "you" now separate from being anxious.

Or maybe you've found ways to become unstuck from or challenge your fearful and anxious-thought patterns. You may even have moments now where you're able to observe your thoughts or feelings without becoming overwhelmed by them.

If you're thinking about your struggle differently, if you're engaging new ways of thinking or behaving, consider yourself victorious. Now keep on doing what's working.

Your Biggest Challenges So Far

What have been your biggest challenges so far? Perhaps you continue to struggle and have not yet seen any noticeable benefit. Or perhaps the improvements feel too small and not impactful enough.

It can feel impossible to keep believing in yourself and your treatment approach when you're not noticing any measurable change. Take a firm look at the facts.

- Are you following the strategies?

- Do you believe the strategies will work?

- Do you believe in yourself and your ability to improve and live the life you deeply desire?

Also, consider if there are specific strategies, or even entire sections of the book, that you find particularly challenging. Reflect on what has been the hardest for you to accept, to take in, and to change. Consider whether you might benefit from additional support to help you with the rougher patches (more on therapy and medication in chapter 12). Give yourself compassion for going toward what's difficult, and for not giving up.

The Road to Progress Isn't Always Straight

Change doesn't unfold in a straight line, although we often believe it should, which is why when we confront setbacks we become self-critical and start to doubt ourselves. This kind of thinking sabotages progress and contributes to us giving up entirely.

The reality is that setbacks and failures along the path to change are inevitable for everyone. Our brains have the miraculous ability to rewire, to grow, to change; however, our brains also cling to what's become habit. This contradictory tension means change does not come immediately or without effort. Sustained change, the kind that really makes a difference, takes time and consistency.

Each time you hit a roadblock, instead of self-criticism and self-defeat, consider the roadblock a signal of your growth and progress. After all, if you were still stuck doing what you've always been doing, you wouldn't have come across a roadblock. When progress on the anxiety-reduction trail stalls, or even halts completely, it means you've likely progressed, more than you imagined, and that's why the setback bothers you. Setbacks are part of your brain's adjustment process. Keep persisting, don't give up, and return to the strategies again and again. It will pay off.

Go
Deeper

Gratitude

Recognizing what we're thankful for increases well-being, contentment, and peace of mind. The negativity bias, as we've seen, is wired into our brain as a survival mechanism. We tend to dwell on, relive, and attempt to problem solve the negative more than the positive. When this process isn't buffered by joy or contentment, we become more anxious.

We can counter the negativity bias easily and in only a few minutes a day. Adopt a daily practice of identifying two or three things that you appreciate. You can write these in your notebook or internally reflect on them. What's important is to bring conscious and deliberate attention to what is going well, or at least okay, in your life or what you feel positively about within yourself.

Building Your New Habits

Once you've been successful with a strategy, take it to the next level. Practice the strategies on multiple occasions across a variety of settings.

For example, if you fear eating out in public, don't decide to just go to the same restaurant with the same friend over and over. Instead, challenge yourself to go to a variety of restaurants and with a variety of people. It's great to become comfortable knowing that you're no longer going to have a panic attack in your local movie theater, but consider branching out to other theaters in nearby towns or even going to a play or a concert. Or if you're working on obsessive thinking, don't just work on it when you're at your place of employment. Work to be mindful, an observer, when home alone, when driving, even when interacting with others. Practice the strategies across a variety of situations/people and you'll eventually start using them instinctively.

The more you act the way you wish you could act, and do the things you used to avoid, and think in the ways that bring peace of mind, the quicker new habits will form and then, before you know it, they'll become automatic.

Exercise: Catch Anxiety Early

Catch anxiety early, before it's left the barn, so to speak, and you'll stop it in its tracks before it becomes too intense to pull back. A way to start catching anxiety early is to develop a quick and easy habit of checking in with yourself. So instead of rushing from task to task, person to person—intentionally STOP. Take time to be mindful of your ongoing experience. Here's how:

- At the end of the day when you arrive home, STOP before entering. Reflect for a few moments; check in with yourself.

- When you end one encounter, STOP. What's going on in your body, your mind? What sensations do you notice?

- When you finish a task, STOP. Reflect on what tinges or shifts might be happening mentally or physically for you. Literally say to yourself, "I want to see you. What's going on in there?"

Tune-Ups and Check-Ins

As you move along your anxiety-recovery path, you may find there are stretches of time when you're no longer deliberately thinking about the strategies. You may feel that you're "in the zone," able to effortlessly manage life's hardships.

Still, even with progress, it's easy for us to go back to old ways of thinking and acting. Consider placing sticky notes in key locations (car, bedroom mirror) or reminders on your digital calendar of the strategies that are working well for you so you keep them top of mind and use them even when you may not feel like you need them. Also, set a reminder on your calendar once or twice a month to review the material in this book and what you've written in your notebook (even if you think you don't need to!).

Goal Setting

Each time you reach a goal, consider the strategies that got you there and if it's possible to expand those strategies to reach even larger goals. For example, perhaps you implemented "total worry time" (page 54) and it worked. Now that you've discovered its effectiveness, consider making it a goal to do this strategy on a daily basis. Or if you recognize that "Watching Your Thoughts" (page 120) works when under stress, consider implementing this strategy every day while driving to work, with or without stress.

Once your overall anxiety level decreases, you'll likely find that you think about your goals in new ways and find deeper, more meaningful, ways to impact your life. And as your well-being increases, the overall picture of the path forward will no longer bring dread but instead pleasure and optimism. You have much to look forward to!

Exercise: What's the Big Picture?

Refocus on the bigger picture in which overall strategies are important to you in maintaining your less-anxious life. These are the strategies that either worked well for you, or are linked to something you care about, like an active social life. Here's a list of some of the things my clients keep in mind. Make a list of your own.

- Physical exercise

- Daily mindfulness

- Physical health

- Live your best life

- Acceptance

- Challenge your thoughts

- Exposure

- Make space for yourself separate from your anxious thoughts

CHAPTER TWELVE

Building Your Support Network

Human connection relieves anxiety. Looking another person in the eye and sharing our vulnerable moments, aspirations, and setbacks soothes our nervous systems. If you've been caught in anxiety's grip for some time, you may not have had the mental space to sustain close family or friendship ties. One-on-one meetings with a therapist or group therapy are ways to start garnering some in-person support. Online anxiety-reduction tools also can be helpful. Sharing your goals, progress, and setbacks with others offers a sturdy brace that will give you encouragement and perspective as you find your way.

Finding a Therapist

Be Calm is for you to use on your own, or with a therapist if you have one. You can find relief on your own if you're persistent and stay with it. However, you will want to participate in psychotherapy if you'd like to accelerate the learning process, deepen your self-awareness, if you have little social support, or if you've implemented the strategies and are not feeling much relief or progress.

Psychotherapy in a sense is a mini laboratory where you can try out your new skills with another human in real time. Unlike your "real" life, the therapeutic life is safe and confidential, and the therapist has no connection with your outside relationships or broader life.

Often, working with a therapist can be tremendously effective in understanding yourself and in developing a support network outside of therapy. The past, in particular unprocessed grief and trauma, has a significant impact on the persistence of anxiety symptoms. Consider weekly psychotherapy to help you work through past trauma and loss that may be impacting your ability to feel sustained relief from anxiety.

As we've seen, anxiety frequently masks other negative emotions that you may be unaware of or have not yet processed. Talking with a therapist can help you uncover those negative emotions and identify what's causing them. Very typically, anxiety lifts when you enter therapy and start the process of exploring your deeper emotions and issues. You may be faced with other complicated emotions, but awareness of them will significantly accelerate the recovery process.

Medication

In some cases, medication along with psychotherapy is the best approach for anxiety reduction. This should be considered only after using the strategies in this book on a consistent basis and meeting with a licensed mental health therapist or clinical psychologist. If you and your therapist believe medication could be helpful, set up an appointment with a psychiatrist. Psychiatrists have specific training in how drugs impact emotions and behavior.

If you decide to try medication, be wary of benzodiazepines and prescription painkillers (including Xanax, Ativan, and Clonazepam/Klonopin). Benzodiazepines and sedatives work right away to bring down anxiety, which provides relief in the moment, but over time it's easy to become dependent on them. Also, if you use sedating medication you will be unmotivated to implement the strategies and your brain will be less able to retain the new ways of dealing with anxiety. And there is a rebound effect when benzodiazepines and painkillers wear off. Anxiety typically comes roaring back in, even stronger, and then you'll feel the immediate need for more of the drug.

Selective serotonin reuptake inhibitors (SSRIs) and serotonin-norepinephrine reuptake inhibitors (SNRIs) are generally more effective for anxiety reduction over the longer term. However, it's essential that you undergo a full assessment with a psychiatrist for an accurate diagnosis and appropriate medication regime.

Getting Referrals

Accessing support, whether with a psychologist, a psychiatrist, or a support group, is a way to enhance your recovery process as you move toward your goal of anxiety reduction. Often, a good place to start is with your general practitioner. Talk to your medical doctor about your symptoms and see if they can refer you to a psychotherapist or clinical psychologist.

Online search engines can also be quite helpful in getting a referral. The Anxiety and Depression Association of America website has a "Find a Therapist" link that will connect you with licensed mental health providers in your geographical area who specialize in the treatment of anxiety. Some of the listed mental health professionals also provide telemental services (online therapy) through video conferencing, phone, or email.

The Social Anxiety Institute website also provides a referral list of treatment providers as well as other resources for lessening social anxiety. The American Psychological Association, a professional organization for psychologists, has an online tool to find a psychologist near you, as does *Psychology Today* where you can read various therapists' profiles to see who might be a good fit.

When searching for a therapist to help you with anxiety symptoms, look for those who are licensed mental health providers or licensed clinical psychologists who specialize in cognitive behavioral therapy, mindfulness, and/or acceptance and commitment therapy. As we've seen, these approaches are well researched and have shown to be effective in the treatment of anxiety disorders.

Online Support

Working on the strategies in a vacuum with no outside influence will not be as effective as if you share what you're doing with the outside world. Whether you talk with trusted friends or family or seek online support makes little difference. However, finding a way to connect with others who also struggle can help you feel more normal and keep the material fresh in your mind.

The National Alliance on Mental Illness (NAMI) is one of the leading mental health organizations in the United States. NAMI supports, advocates, and educates on behalf of the mentally ill and their families. The NAMI website offers support regarding a range of mental health experiences, as well as what it is like to live with the stigma of mental illness.

The Anxiety and Depression Association of America has an online anxiety and depression support group where you can connect with people all over the world who cope with anxiety. You can join this group anonymously through the online app or through subscribing.

One positive step to take is to sign up and simply peruse ongoing conversations to help you feel connected to others struggling with similar symptoms. Over time, you may become more and more comfortable initiating your own discussions.

The National Suicide Prevention Lifeline (1-800-273-8255) provides free confidential support, 24 hours a day, seven days a week for people in crisis and in need of immediate intervention.

Support Groups

Group therapy is extremely effective in lessening anxiety symptoms. In fact, for some people, group therapy is more impactful than individual therapy. Group therapy works because it challenges our ideas that we're alone in our suffering and are somehow "bad" or "less than" others as a result. This experience reduces shame and isolation and also helps with the idea of accepting anxiety while you continue to live your life.

Communicating and connecting in a group therapy setting often helps people develop self-awareness around their role(s) in social relationships. While in the group, a person may act out a role that they use to manage their anxiety in real life, i.e., overly friendly, withdrawn, very inquisitive, constantly talking, dismissive. Group members typically reflect on the roles they notice and provide one another with feedback. Because group therapy is not real life and is confidential, it feels safe for people to process such feedback. As a result, they become more flexible or even adopt other roles in the group that will eventually extend to their real-life relationships.

In addition, when we're in an anxious state, adrenaline can take over. It can be hard to know what we feel deep down, let alone find the words to express what we're feeling. Yet, anxiety typically decreases when we're able to talk with others. Group therapy is a type of exposure in that you'll probably feel anxious at moments. At the same time, it's a nonthreatening place for you to become more skillful at knowing what you're feeling, when you're feeling it, and becoming comfortable expressing it.

Finding a Group

If you decide that group therapy is a treatment approach you'd like to try, and you have an individual therapist, consider asking your therapist if they know of a group that would be a good fit for you. Alternatively, there is a "Find a Support Group" feature on the Anxiety and Depression Association of America website as well as the *Psychology Today* website.

Keep in mind there are two common types of group therapies. "Process-oriented" groups are led by a therapist, but generally the therapist lets the group members steer the discussion. Process groups are about the group members' experiences of what they're observing, feeling, or want to discuss.

"Psychoeducational" groups also are led by a therapist but the therapist takes on an instructor role. Psychoeducational groups are helpful when you're looking to gain specific skills in some area of your life or functioning. In this case an anxiety psychoeducational group might discuss coping skills and strategies.

Starting a Group

As we've seen, anxiety is an extremely prevalent issue for many people. If you're looking for an anxiety therapy group in your local area and can't find one, chances are others are, too.

If you decide to start a group, think carefully about how you wish to structure it, what kinds of members you're targeting for the group (only anxiety, anxiety and other mood issues, relationship issues), and who will be the leader. Consider if you want this to be a process-oriented or more of an information-sharing group. It's also important to think through group therapy rules. It's typically helpful not to have a group with family members or people who know one another very well because it reduces anonymity and the comfort that comes from anonymity. Confidentiality among group members is key to feeling safe and open, which is what helps people grow.

Staying the Course

Like many things in life, success in your pursuit of anxiety reduction and internal peace takes patience, adaptability, and perseverance. Of course, anxiety is unpleasant and you'd like it to stop as quickly as possible. However, habits take practice to form and they take practice to break. Compassionately remind yourself that there's nothing wrong with you if you feel that your recovery isn't moving as fast as you'd like. And just because it's taking time doesn't mean you won't get better.

Allow yourself to adjust the strategies for your personal brand of anxiety symptoms. One strategy may work for a while, but it's important to try new ones so you stay challenged and keep growing. As your symptoms improve, the anxiety will likely change and present itself differently. You will need to adjust and bring new skills into your repertoire. If the strategies aren't working or are going only so far, then consider individual psychotherapy or group therapy. Some people do both. If therapy doesn't work on its own, consider combining psychotherapy and medication.

And, most importantly, whatever you do, don't give up! Allow yourself to pick the work back up again and again. Believe in the process. Your work will pay off in the form of a brighter future.

Resources

Online

Anxiety and Depression Association of America (adaa.org)

Social Anxiety Institute (socialanxietyinstitute.org)

American Psychological Association (apa.org)

National Alliance on Mental Illness (nami.org)

National Suicide Prevention Lifeline (1-800-273-8255)

Headspace: Meditation app

Calm: Meditation and sleep app

Further Reading

Antony, M. M. and Swinson, R. P. (2009). *When Perfect Isn't Good Enough: Strategies for Coping with Perfectionism.* Oakland, CA: New Harbinger.

Bourne, E. J. (2015). *The Anxiety and Phobia Workbook* (6th ed.). Oakland, CA: New Harbinger.

Carbonell, D. A. (2016). *The Worry Trick: How Your Brain Tricks You into Expecting the Worst and What You Can Do About It.* Oakland, CA: New Harbinger.

Collard, P. (2014). *Little Book of Mindfulness: 10 Minutes a Day to Less Stress, More Peace.* Colorado: Gaia.

Hanh, Thich Nhat. (1999). *The Miracle of Mindfulness: An Introduction to the Practice of Meditation.* Boston: Beacon Press.

Hayes, S. C. (2005). *Get Out of Your Mind and Into Your Life: The New Acceptance and Commitment Therapy.* Oakland, CA: New Harbinger.

Knaus, W. J. (2014). *The Cognitive Behavioral Workbook for Anxiety: A Step-By-Step Program* (2nd ed.). Oakland, CA: New Harbinger.

Pittman, C. M. and Karle, E. M. (2015). *Rewire Your Anxious Brain: How to Use the Neuroscience of Fear to End Anxiety, Panic, and Worry.* Oakland, CA: New Harbinger.

References

Baltazar, N. C., Shutts, K., and Kinzler, K. D. (2012). "Children Show Heightened Memory for Threatening Social Actions." *Journal of Experimental Child Psychology*, 112(1): 102–10.

Boswell, J. F., Thompson-Hollands, J., Farchione, T. J., and Barlow, D. H. (2014). "Intolerance of Uncertainty: A Common Factor in the Treatment of Emotional Disorders." *Journal of Clinical Psychology*, 69(6): 630–45.

Craske, M. G., Treanor, M., Conway, C., Zbozinek, T., and Vervliet, B. (2014). "Maximizing Exposure Therapy: An Inhibitory Learning Approach." *Behaviour Research and Therapy*, 58: 10–23.

Culpepper, L. (2009). "Generalized Anxiety Disorder and Medical Illness." *Journal of Clinical Psychiatry*, 70, 20–24.

Jackson, M. C., Wu, C. Y., Linden, D. E., and Raymond, J. E. (2009). "Enhanced Visual Short-Term Memory for Angry Faces." *Journal of Experimental Psychology: Human Perception and Performance*, 35(2): 363–74.

Jakubovski, E. and Bloch, M. H. (2016). "Anxiety Disorder-Specific Predictors of Treatment Outcome in the Coordinated Anxiety Learning and Management (CALM) Trial." *Psychiatry Quarterly*, 87(3): 445–64.

Katon, W. J., Richardson, L., Lozano, P., and McCauley, E. (2004). "The Relationship of Asthma and Anxiety Disorders." *Psychosomatic Medicine*, 66(3): 349–55.

McCallie, M. S., Blum, C. M., and Hood, C. J. (2006). "Progressive Muscle Relaxation." *Journal of Human Behavior in the Social Environment*, 13(3): 51–66.

Missig, G., Mei, L., Vizzard, M. A., et al. (2017). "Parabrachial PACAP Activation of Amygdala Endosomal ERK Signaling Regulates the Emotional Component of Pain." *Biological Psychiatry*, 81(8): 671–82.

Roest, A. M., Martens, E. J., de Jonge P., and Denollet, J. (2010). "Anxiety and Risk of Incident Coronary Heart Disease: A Meta-Analysis." *Journal of American College of Cardiology*, Jun 29; 56(1): 38–46.

Wegner, D. M., Schneider, D. J., Carter, S. R., and White, T. L. (1987). "Paradoxical Effects of Thought Suppression." *Journal of Personality and Social Psychology*, 53(1): 5–13.

Willgoss, T. G. and Yohannes, A. M. (2013). "Anxiety Disorders in Patients with COPD: A Systematic Review." *Respiratory Care*, 58(5): 858–66.

Index

About the Author

 Jill P. Weber, PhD, is a clinical psychologist in private practice in Washington, D.C. She is also a psychology author and a speaker. Dr. Weber works with teenagers, individuals, and couples managing varying degrees of anxiety from panic attacks, generalized anxiety, and life stress. Dr. Weber uses a combined approach of cognitive behavioral therapy, mindfulness, and acceptance techniques when working with anxiety symptoms. She writes a blog for *Psychology Today* and has appeared as a psychology expert in various media outlets including *USA Today, Washington Post, Nightline, U.S. News & World Report,* and CNN. Dr. Weber is the author of *Having Sex, Wanting Intimacy: Why Women Settle for One-Sided Relationships* and the Relationship Formula series including the titles *Breaking Up and Divorce 5 Steps, Building Self-Esteem 5 Steps, Toxic Love 5 Steps,* and *Getting Close to Others 5 Steps.* For more information, see www.DrJillWeber.com.

Printed in the USA
CPSIA information can be obtained
at www.ICGtesting.com
CBHW040713120324
5247CB00005B/16

9 781641 522083